Autistic
Rhapsody

Autistic Rhapsody

Alan Griswold

AUTISTIC RHAPSODY

iUniverse books may be ordered through booksellers or by contacting:

iUniverse
1663 Liberty Drive
Bloomington, IN 47403
www.iuniverse.com
844-349-9409

Because of the dynamic nature of the Internet, any web addresses or links contained in this book may have changed since publication and may no longer be valid. The views expressed in this work are solely those of the author and do not necessarily reflect the views of the publisher, and the publisher hereby disclaims any responsibility for them.

Any people depicted in stock imagery provided by Getty Images are models, and such images are being used for illustrative purposes only. Certain stock imagery © Getty Images.

ISBN: 978-1-6632-5233-3 (sc)
ISBN: 978-1-6632-5234-0 (e)

Library of Congress Control Number: 2023907391

Print information available on the last page.

iUniverse rev. date: 04/20/2023

Sections

1. Introduction: The Riddle of Humanity

The human species, our species, is extraordinary. There are perhaps an endless variety of ways to justify that statement. Consider for instance the immense catalog of human construction: skyscrapers, bridges, radio towers, electrical grids, millions of cars, millions of houses—a list that barely begins to scratch the surface. Or contemplate the effective manner in which the members of our species can migrate and connect, far-ranging travel by train, ship and airplane, opening personal vistas onto essentially the entire planet. Or ponder the efficient means by which we now communicate on a daily basis, including hundreds of thousands of messages—written, spoken and visual—hastening around the globe each and every second, the lifeblood of businesses and so many vibrant institutions, from schools to governments to social networks. Or think of the unfathomably rich scientific knowledge we have come to possess regarding our surrounding world: relativity, quantum theory, the periodic table, evolution, genetics, to name only the most basic components of our understanding. Or reflect upon the entire tableau of the creative arts—so many dazzling instances of literature, music, painting and more, artifacts that entertain us, uplift us, and hold a mirror to ourselves.

Of course there are problems and challenges too—poverty, war, environmental destruction—and it remains unclear whether the glory of humanity might eventually (and all too suddenly) become the tragedy of humanity. But those challenges cannot negate the enormity of the transformation this species has already wrought. It is a transformation that began not that long ago—not that long ago, that is, on any biological

1

or geological timescale. It is a transformation that arose from a narrowly confined set of climates and habitats in which the members of this species lived out their lives as nothing more than simple beasts, no different in nature and behavior from the wild animals we observe today. The history of that transformation—from the first use of fire and clothing, through the domestication of livestock and grains, through the pyramids and the Parthenon, through the Copernican and Industrial Revolutions, to the multifaceted and far-reaching discoveries of the twentieth century—that history alone would be jaw-dropping enough. But perhaps more stunning still is the realization that this transformation continues unabated through the present day, and indeed, as appears to have always been the case, it continues at a steadily accelerating pace.

Everywhere one looks, one sees a human environment overflowing with the most amazing complexities, an environment brimming with intricacies that would have been unimaginable in any previous era. And everywhere one looks, one sees humans nimbly navigating those complexities and intricacies, displaying skills that would have been inconceivable to any prior age. Watch the child poking her fingers into her electronic learning toy. Marvel at the teenager high-fiving his friend in virtual space. Stand over the shoulder of the animator constructing landscapes more detailed and more dynamic than any actual landscape could manage to sustain. And listen to the men and women clacking at their keyboards, programming machines to perform a broad assortment of tasks, from the purest forms of drudgery to the most delicate of medical procedures. We find ourselves literally awash in an environmental and behavioral transformation, one that bathes us ever more thoroughly with each passing day, and one that has removed us far far away from our former purely animal selves.

The odd thing is, we humans are mostly immune to any sense of awe and wonderment regarding our own species. Having been born into these circumstances, having learned from a young age to speak, to read, to write, to calculate; having driven a car, having taken airplane flights, having traversed hundreds of shops, offices and boulevards; having rocked the town in the latest fashion, having anesthetized and healed our broken bones, having watched rockets shooting into space; having been exposed to all this and much much more, we are not so apt to be astounded by such events and artifacts—they are, after all, simply the everyday material of our everyday lives. Even the novelties, even those rich changes that still rain down upon us on a nearly continuous basis, even this nascent fuel of our ongoing human transformation, even this manages to escape our amazement. Electronic infant toys, virtual reality, clamorous animations, robotics—these may be relatively new to us, but let's face it, they are already becoming routine.

If we want to capture a sense of amazement regarding our own species and to experience an awareness of just how outrageously atypical humanity has become, we need to gain some context and perspective. We need to take a step back from ourselves as it were, disengage from our everyday lives, and view the human transformation through a lens of time and space, through a lens of detachment, like an audience watching a movie. As a hint of what I mean here, there is an Italian animated film from 1976, *Allegro Non Troppo*, that contains a sequence providing an impressionistic version of the type of transformational portrayal we seek. The sequence begins with a soft drink bottle tossed onto a barren planet, with the planet's first cells of life germinating and multiplying within the bottle's residue liquid, the cells eventually slopping past the bottle's opening and onto the planet's surface. What follows is a whimsical march of evolution and progress, from simple and strange organisms to ever more complex and ever more numerous organisms, including a mammal-like creature that transforms into a primate-like creature that transforms into a hominin-like creature. Thus from the quietude of its beginning, the planet grows increasingly more crowded, more dynamic, more frightful, more sublime, culminating at last in an immense eruption of human-built structures, dominating the once barren landscape—and all this set to the strains of Ravel's *Bolero*, from its hauntingly simple opening melody to its overwhelmingly crashing crescendo.

Allegro Non Troppo is of course more fanciful than accurate, but today we do have access to a similar portrayal, one that is not fanciful but is instead scientific, comprehensive, and germane to the purpose at hand. I am speaking of David Christian's notion of Big History, especially as set forth in his approachable book *Origin Story: A Big History of Everything*. Big History describes events that have taken place from the Big Bang (the beginning of time) through the present day, and highlights the major transformations—*thresholds*, they are termed—that have shaped our world across that expanse, such as the formation of the chemical elements, the emergence of galaxies and solar systems, the genesis of single-celled life and the not-so-easy transition to multicellular big life, and then the advent of humans and all the stages of that species' remarkable transformation. Big History analyzes these events through the lenses of complexity, energy and entropy, and through a search for the presence of goldilocks conditions, the just-right circumstances that allow for a spawning of the next big transition. Big History is a fifty-thousand foot view overlooking a 13.8-billion year process. For humans, Big History provides a large dose of context and perspective.

To that end, *Origin Story* is noteworthy in three important respects, each of which will warrant some further discussion:

1. **Timeline and timescale**. *Origin Story* outlines the latest scientific knowledge and evidence regarding the timeline of the cosmic and planetary events covered in its pages, and furthermore the book offers a sense of scale for that timeline. A sense of scale is critical here, both for an understanding of the immense temporal expanse that took place before the arrival of humans, as well as for an appreciation of the relative sliver of time during which the human species has achieved the entirety of its transformational turn.

2. **Human thresholds**. There are eight major thresholds enumerated by Big History, the last three of which are human generated. It would be tempting to chalk up this high percentage of human discussion to an anthropocentric bias, but *Origin Story* provides ample argument and abundant evidence that the human transitions are indeed seismic, unprecedented, and on a level with the other cosmic and evolutionary milestones on the list.

3. **Impetus to human reassessment**. Nearly all the factual evidence presented within *Origin Story* represents scientific knowledge crystallized only since around the middle of the twentieth century, with much of that knowledge directly challenging the traditional ways in which humans have perceived themselves. The old models, still entrenched within the collective consciousness, no longer apply.

The first respect in which *Origin Story* is noteworthy is in its handling of cosmological, geological and biological timelines and in its acknowledgement that human thinking is still trying to adjust to the enormous scale that underlies these timelines. When Charles Darwin's *On the Origin of Species* was first published in 1859, it disquieted the public not only for its evolutionary theories and their implication for human origins, it created unease also for its suggestion that the age of the earth and universe was immense, perhaps hundreds of millions of years. In the mid-nineteenth century, it was still hardly conceivable that the interval of prehistory could utterly dwarf that of the known human era. But as scientific evidence continued to mount over the next century and a half, and as that evidence became more and more precise, Darwin's suggestion proved to be inaccurate only to the extent of its underestimation. Easy to conceive or not, the age of the known human era turns out to be as nothing compared to the age of the universe.

By the late twentieth century, radiometric and cosmological dating techniques had progressed to the point that confirmed and accepted timelines were taking shape for the cosmos, for the solar system, for life, and for humans. Agreement crystallized around the notion that the universe had started with a singularity event, the Big Bang, approximately 13.8 billion years ago, followed by a series of cosmological and biological milestones that bridged the gap to the present day. *Origin Story* charts these milestones and their approximate dates, most of which are reproduced in the following table:

Event	Approximate Date
Big Bang	13.8 billion years ago
First Forging of Chemical Elements	13.2 billion years ago
Formation of the Solar System	4.5 billion years ago
Earliest Life on Earth	3.8 billion years ago
First Large Life on Earth	600 million years ago
Dinosaurs Extincted by Asteroid Event	65 million years ago
Hominin Branch Splits from Other Great Apes	7 million years ago
Appearance of Homo sapiens	200,000 years ago
Farming and Civilizations Begin	10,000 years ago
Scientific and Industrial Revolutions Begin	400 years ago
Humans Land on the Moon	50 years ago

13.8 billion years is an extremely long period of time, longer than we humans can easily grasp and internalize, given the length of an average lifespan. For that matter, two hundred thousand years is also an extremely long period of time, perhaps a tad more fathomable than 13.8 billion years, but still outside the ken of normal human experience. So it is perhaps difficult for us to truly appreciate that there is a significant difference between the two.

To help its readers absorb the timescales involved, *Origin Story* offers an adjusted timeline in which all the approximate dates for events are divided by one billion years, meaning that on the adjusted scale, the Big Bang is assumed to have occurred only about 13 years and 9 months ago. This certainly makes it easier for us to fathom the interval, although it might give the mistaken impression that the event is not that far removed, an impression that can be dispelled by the realization that on the adjusted timeline, the average human lifespan plays out over a mere two seconds. Accordingly, the following table repeats the one from above, but now with the approximate dates adjusted by a division of one billion years:

Event	Approximate Date / 1 Billion Years
Big Bang	13 years and 9 months ago
First Forging of Chemical Elements	13 years and 2 months ago
Formation of the Solar System	4 years and 6 months ago
Earliest Life on Earth	3 years and 9 months ago
First Large Life on Earth	7 months ago
Dinosaurs Extincted by Asteroid Event	24 days ago
Hominin Branch Splits from Other Great Apes	2 and 1/2 days ago
Appearance of Homo sapiens	1 hour and 40 minutes ago
Farming and Civilizations Begin	5 minutes ago
Scientific and Industrial Revolutions Begin	12 seconds ago
Humans Land on the Moon	1 and 1/2 seconds ago

These comparisons help make it clear that cosmological, biological and human events play out on very different timescales. Cosmological forces are enormous not just in their spatial scope but also in their temporal reach, with significant events typically measured and compared in billions of years. Of the 13.8 billion years that have passed from the Big Bang to the present moment, around 67% of that time had already been spent when the sun and planets of our solar system first came into being, and another 5% would be consumed waiting for the first simple life forms to appear on the planet Earth.

By comparison, the biological/evolutionary timescale is a bit more compact and dynamic, although still lengthy in absolute terms, with significant events more typically measured in millions or perhaps hundreds of millions of years. Even here, leaps of complexity apparently do not come quickly or easily, for on Earth microbial single-celled life remained without partner for around three billion years, consuming another 22% of the overall timeline, leaving only around 6% for the era of multicellular organisms and big life (that is, the size and type of flora and fauna we experience on Earth today).

By comparison again, human events have played out in a time frame that appears to be essentially negligible relative to those of its predecessors. The hominin line has been around for only about 0.05% of the time of the universe, and *Homo sapiens*, our species, has been in existence for only about 0.0015% of the overall timeline. And although the exact beginning of the human transformation remains somewhat uncertain, the first unmistakable and abundant evidence for the turn that would put this species on a path clearly different from that of all the other species, this dates to around fifty to one hundred thousand years ago, meaning that nearly every significant event of the human transformation has taken place over an interval covering only about 0.0005% of the universe's timeline, a chronological splinter that would be thought hardly significant in almost any other context.

The second respect in which *Origin Story* is noteworthy is in its straightforward demonstration that the human-generated transitions of the last one hundred thousand years or so are of a similar nature and carry similar impact as the cosmological and biological transitions that went before.

Big History enumerates eight different thresholds—fundamental changes that have reshaped a critical aspect of our world: 1. Big Bang Origins, 2. Stars and Galaxies, 3. Chemical Elements and Molecules, 4. Solar System and Earth, 5. Life, 6. Human Difference, 7. Agriculture, 8. Modern Revolution. A threshold is signified by several telltale characteristics. The first and perhaps most obvious of these is a pronounced leap in complexity, often going hand in hand with a more focused and more enriched use of energy. An increase in complexity runs counter to the effects of entropy, the tendency for energy and systems to become more ineffective, more diffuse and more random over time. Entropy is the default condition of the universe, and so relentless is its impact that it will ultimately, in a distant future, become the final fate of the universe. But against this incessant pull towards entropy, eddies of great complexity can still occur, localized and chaos-defying leaps of increased pattern, increased structure and increased form, indicators of a new threshold. Another characteristic of thresholds is their so-called goldilocks effects, the just-right conditions that make it possible for the next leap in complexity to occur—conditions that are not too hot and not too cold, not too dense and not too sparse, not too oxygen rich and not too oxygen poor, etc.

The first five thresholds—the non-human thresholds—demonstrate these concepts. The Big Bang and its aftermath, chaotic though it was,

was more complex and more energy infused than the nothingness that apparently gave birth to it. Then as temperatures cooled to just the right degree and gravity tugged by just the right amount, clusters of stars and galaxies began to form, more organized than the tumultuous foam from which they came. Then in certain dying stars, of just the right magnitude and of just the right composition, the heavier chemical elements were fused and exploded into space, giving us carbon, oxygen, and the other elements of the periodic table, as well as all their molecular potential—an enormous increase in chemical complexity that undergirds our physical world today. Finally, in certain star systems, such as our own, and on certain planets, such as planet Earth, conditions came together in just the right way to support yet another leap in chemical and dynamic complexity—the leap to biological life. And on Earth at least, life itself seems to have contained an impetus towards an ever-greater complexity, an ever-greater use of energy, with single-celled life leading eventually to multicellular life and finally to big life—a burgeoning cauldron of evolutionary forces.

These first five thresholds had produced the state of affairs that could be found on Earth around two hundred thousand years ago, and it was into this state of affairs that *Homo sapiens* emerged. According to Big History, what then followed were three more thresholds in rapid succession, all human inspired. But we should probably pause at this moment and ask ourselves first, is this really a valid depiction of what took place? Three entire thresholds dedicated solely to the human species? Are we sure this is not just an instance of anthropocentric bias? Humans have a natural tendency to be enamored of their own species and of what that species has done, and scientists and academicians are as susceptible to this tendency as anyone else. So is this perhaps the explanation for the self-assignment of three entire thresholds to the human species, is this maybe just a case of David Christian running amok, unable to suppress his admiration for his own kind?

To help answer that question, note that biological life, despite its abundant variety, has a certain predictability to it. In the animal kingdom, for instance, due to the constant evolutionary pressure to survive and to procreate, each organism channels its efforts into just a few select activities: eating, drinking, avoiding danger, sexual rivalry, mating, fostering young. You may have noticed that every documentary that chronicles an animal species follows essentially the same plot line: the search for food and water, the warding off of predators, sexual rituals, the fragile course from birth to adulthood—and then the cycle starts all over again. Thus, animal behavior remains remarkably stable and consistent, across time and across species. The lions, catfish, crows, beavers, etc. of today behave essentially the same as did the lions, catfish, crows, beavers, etc. from hundreds of thousands of years ago. And on the African savanna, around two hundred thousand years ago, the earliest instances of *Homo sapiens* could have been anticipated to be no different.

And yet by fifty to one hundred thousand years ago, the evidence was quickly mounting that this species was in fact unlike all the rest. Control of fire, specialized tools, cave art, larger social structures (pointing to an almost certain use of abstract language). By ten thousand years ago, the human difference was unmistakable. The population was increasing at an unprecedented rate, the use of environmental resources was taking a quantum leap. The species had by now spread out around the globe, covering nearly all of Africa and Eurasia, and having forayed for the first time into Australia and the Americas. *Homo sapiens* had extincted—other than some small DNA assimilation—all the other hominin lines. *Homo sapiens* had extincted many of the larger mammals as well. Tools, weapons, art, cooking, clothing, abstract communication, a more concentrated use of energy—these were undeniable escalations in behavioral complexity, escalations for which no other species, at no other time, had even given a hint. A new threshold had indeed been crossed.

And humans were not finished. Around ten thousand years ago, in the vicinity and ideal conditions of the Fertile Crescent, the species began to develop agricultural techniques, domesticating certain grains and unleashing their enriched energy, and harnessing certain animals and employing their augmented power. Farming paved the way to larger social structures, to what would eventually become civilizations. Farming spawned an outpouring of construction, from colossal examples such as the pyramids and the Acropolis, to more humble yet indispensable instances, such as thousands and thousands of abodes. Ships began to sail the seas, carts began to cross the land, speech began to be written down. By the year 1600, the human difference had turned into a human domination.

And yet humans were still not finished. Around four hundred years ago, another revolution began to take hold, another massive jump in world complexity. Spurred by scientific and mathematical methods, such as those epitomized by Newtonian mechanics, and powered by industrial invention, such as the burning of fossil fuels, humans began to cram their surroundings with an unprecedented depth and breadth of structure: railroads, automobiles, airplanes; factories, terminals, stadiums; radios, televisions, computers; and now so many massive and skyscrapered cities, all stuffed with plumbing, traffic and electricity, intricate dances of infrastructure reaching to the clouds. By the twentieth century, the extent of human knowledge was bumping against what was surely the universe's limits: subatomic particles, relativity, genetics. And perhaps a bit on the more ominous side, if there were to remain any doubt about the energies now employable by this species, note that at one irritable push of a button, we can potentially annihilate every organism on the planet Earth, bringing to an abrupt halt what has been more than a three-and-a-half-billion-year process.

Homo sapiens is not a normal life form. Even with all anthropocentric bias duly noted, the fact remains that the human species has utterly transcended the evolutionary boundaries that have confined every other instance of biological life. Humanity has earned all the attention it gets.

The third respect in which *Origin Story* is noteworthy is that it establishes a new narrative regarding humanity—a new narrative about humanity's environment, a new narrative about humanity's origins, and a new narrative about humanity's ongoing history. The first glimpses into this new narrative were becoming apparent in the nineteenth century, but it was not until the last half of the twentieth century that the story emerged fully into view, and thus we find ourselves now, early in the twenty-first century, still in a period of readjustment, still coming to grips with the new paradigm. But it should also be obvious by now that this new narrative does not align to the manner in which humans have traditionally regarded themselves, meaning that a self-reassessment is becoming quickly overdue.

There have been two well-established traditions for explaining humanity and for describing humanity's place within the world. For convenience I will label the first of these approaches as the *religious tradition*, and I will label the second approach as the *philosophical tradition*.

There are probably as many religious origin stories as there are religions, but they do tend to share a common theme. A divine force, often called God, creates the world and its contents—the earth and the heavens, the rocks and the streams, the plants and the animals. Then furthermore, God *specially* creates humans, the specialness intended to account for all the uniquely human traits—intelligence, language, inventiveness and all the rest. And because humans are special and because the world serves as their domain, it is usually stated or implied that the world was created shortly before, or alongside, the very first humans. In some religious traditions, creation is seen as God's one and final act, but in many, God continues to play a role in ongoing events, such as when he sends his only begotten son.

It is not my intention to disparage religious thought. I have met too many people who will mindlessly dismiss religion as being irrational and backwards, entirely misapprehending the subject. No other animal species has ever had a religious notion, and neither did humans for a very long time. Religious thinking is evidence of a striving for greater understanding, it is a signpost on the road towards human progress. And furthermore, a study of religious history will reveal that religions have tended to become more sophisticated, more complex, and more comprehensive with time, fitting into the overall theme of human transformation and human advancement. Any honest effort towards religious striving is to be treated with utmost respect (just as any selfish push towards fundamentalism is to be confronted with utmost reproach).

Nonetheless, the religious tradition does not hold. The world was not created alongside humans—in fact, the universe had been in existence for nearly an eternity before humans came along. The world has not served solely as a human domain—in the spatial-temporal continuum, humans barely mark a trace. And as for specialness, humans began as animals, they were once beasts like so many others—intelligence, language, inventiveness and all the rest, in the beginning these were nowhere to be found. But if all this seems a bit too humbling, humans can take some comfort in the one apparent compensation, that they in fact owe divinity not a thing in the way of debt for all that humanity has now become. Intelligence, language, inventiveness and all the rest—these have been entirely human forged.

Turning to the philosophical tradition, it seems to have arisen to some extent out of a dissatisfaction with the religious tradition, as well as out of a dissatisfaction with the turmoil of human change. In the philosophical tradition, a creator is not the primary focus. Instead, the world and its events are measured against the apotheosis of a natural or ideal state, a state that is essentially timeless, a state in which rationality preferably reigns supreme. Thus, humans are special in this tradition too, for they alone are endowed with an innate faculty of reason, and the challenge of human experience is to overcome the strife, the confusion, the disruption of ordinary life, to attain or to regain a rational equilibrium, to establish a well-ordered stasis. Such ideas were fundamental to both Plato and Aristotle, and their influence reached forward into the Age of Enlightenment, where Descartes, Leibniz, Voltaire, Rousseau and others could refine and foster the tradition. So persuasive has been this approach in the shaping of how humans have perceived themselves, it should be noted that even a philosopher such as Kant, so willing to fathom and to question almost every other human concept, was nonetheless willing to accept an innate faculty of reason as simply a given.

And yet as with the religious tradition, the philosophical tradition does not hold. The natural state of a human is to be purely an animal, a human's equilibrium condition is to be evolution bound on the African plains. Not a stasis, but instead a dynamic artificial construction has been the driver for vaulting this species to its more ideal place, and thus it is the turmoil of human change, the turmoil of human transformation—the strife, the confusion, the disruption—it is to these we owe the formation of our not-so-innate reason.

The facts as we currently understand them are these, this is the new narrative:

Around 13.8 billion years ago, our world began in a tumultuous burst of energy. As that world expanded and cooled, stars and galaxies were formed, followed by the chemical elements. On the planets of some of these star systems, conditions would allow for life, and this is what happened on the planet Earth, over three and one half billion years ago. Biological life on Earth remained simple for quite some time, but eventually evolved to something more complex, to the types of plants and animals we are more familiar with today. Sometimes conditions were chaotic for life—asteroid strikes, temperature swings, volcanic eruptions—producing mass extinctions followed by evolutionary explosions. But at other times conditions were more stable, allowing evolution to take a more gradual course, and it was during the most recent stable period that hominins first emerged, leading eventually to *Homo sapiens*.

If those earliest *Homo sapiens* individuals possessed any of the behaviors of human modernity, those behaviors must have been inchoate at best. Life for those earliest *Homo sapiens* individuals was focused almost entirely on survival and procreation, just as to be expected. But it was not too long thereafter that the signs emerged that this species was in fact extraordinary. From life as simple hunter-gatherers humans quickly turned to becoming world conquerors, reconstructing their environment almost constantly along the way. Populations increased by orders of magnitude, geographical expansion extended around the globe. Farming, writing, civilization, seafaring, science, industry—in a steady acceleration, humans kept building on what they had built before. By the twenty-first century humans had practically obliterated nature from their view, substituting in its wake a multitude of sprawling, towering monuments to artificial pattern, structure and form. Behaviors that were once evolution bound had now reached an almost unlimited expression: language, computation, constant innovation. And so deeply had this species now plumbed the depths of its surrounding world that it was on the verge of conquering the fundamental building blocks of the universe, and the fundamental building blocks of life itself.

The facts as we currently understand them are these, we must see ourselves in the light of this new narrative.

There is, however, an irony at the heart of this new narrative. As deeply as humans have now seen into so many different aspects of their world—biology, physics, chemistry, mathematics, logic—there is one subject, perhaps the most important subject of them all, for which this species has yet to achieve even the most basic understanding. That one subject is humanity itself. That is to say, humans do not as yet understand themselves, and they do not as yet understand what has engendered their remarkable history.

Note how during the last several hundred years—the era of Big History's final threshold, the modern revolution—humanity has forged a complete revision of its understanding regarding almost every feature and every process underlying the observable world. For instance, humans have long gazed at the moon, the stars, the planets, the other contents of the cosmos, have observed the patterns and observed the aberrations, and have asked questions about what is going on. Why the regularity? Why the aberrations? What are the relationships between all these heavenly bodies? What drives the celestial dance? Over the years there have been suggestions, declarations, arguments, discussion, and occasionally a bit of insight, but it was not until the modern era that our knowledge turned deep, sophisticated and effective, and now we have Newton's laws of motion and gravity, and Einstein's relativity, to help us navigate our way around. Humans have long pondered the material objects of their surrounding world—the rocks, the water, the air—have observed each substance's unique properties, have noticed the combinatory changes these substances often undergo, and have asked questions about what is taking place. What are these things made of? Why are some of them liquid and some of them solid? Why do they combine in such transformative and fiery ways? What drives the material dance? Over the years there have been suggestions, declarations, arguments, discussion, and occasionally a bit of insight, but it was not until the modern era that our knowledge turned deep, sophisticated and effective, and now we have atomic and quantum theory to help us comprehend the scene. Humans have long contemplated the immense variety of life—trees, flowers, fish, insects, birds—have watched each organism's natural behaviors, have witnessed the births and witnessed the deaths, and have asked questions about how to explain these events. Why are there so many different kinds? What is the purpose behind each organism's behavior? From where do these organisms come? What drives the organic dance? Over the years there have been suggestions, declarations, arguments, discussion, and occasionally a bit of insight, but it was not until the modern era that our knowledge turned deep, sophisticated and effective, and now we have evolutionary theory and genetics to help us clarify the living drama.

But note this too, that humans have also long observed themselves. Humans are aware that they are in many respects just like all the other living creatures—humans must eat and drink, avoid danger, have sex and procreate, and rear their young. Humans are also aware that they are utterly unique—language, intelligence, innovation. And humans have asked questions about how did this situation come to be. Why are we both the same and different from all the other animals? From what do we derive our unique abilities? Is there a purpose to what we have constructed all around us, and what do we do now? What drives the human dance? Over the years there have been suggestions, declarations, arguments, discussion, and occasionally a bit of insight, but…alas, even in the modern era, there has been only minimal progress.

We do know now more about human history, that temporally speaking this history has been minuscule compared to everything that went before, and that consequentially speaking this history has been nothing short of epic. We know now that we began purely as animals, and that once the transition was set into motion, the pace of change turned into a constructive acceleration, leading to the outrageously altered circumstances we find ourselves in today. But these are only descriptions, they are not insights into what has shaped the human dance. These are inventories of what has taken place, they are not elucidations that can help us understand. When it comes to explaining the processes underlying human events, when it comes to seeing deeply, sophisticatedly and effectively into the features that have defined the human transformation, we recognize that there are no equivalents to the laws of motion and gravity, to relativity; no equivalents to the periodic table, to quantum theory; no equivalents to evolution, to genetics. Humans do not as yet understand themselves.

This overarching question regarding the human transition—how did humans change from pure animal to what humans have become today, what processes underlie this unprecedented and powerful transformation—this is what I call the riddle of humanity. As a scientific question it is indeed important, perhaps the most important scientific question yet to have received much of an answer. But the importance of the question goes beyond just the demands of scientific inquiry, for it is also a question that has implications for the future course of humankind.

If we could put ourselves beside those earliest farmers in the Fertile Crescent and ask them to predict what the future would be like in another ten thousand years, we recognize that we would be setting them an impossible task. Airplanes, electricity, calculus, the internet—hardly a single concept that defines the current age would have yet to reach those farmers' ken. And are we in a similar position today ourselves, trying to anticipate our own future? True, if we could assume another ten thousand years of transformation similar to the ten thousand years that have gone before, then indeed we might expect a world full of artifacts and events that we could not possibly conceive today. But in a certain sense, this exercise seems strange and futile. The accelerating pace of human change, although bringing with it a host of technological marvels and environmental understandings, has also brought with it the looming consequences of a runaway recklessness—widespread extinction of many species, proliferation of weapons of mass destruction, rapid deterioration of the global climate. At times it seems unlikely that humanity will make it through the next ten years, let alone the next ten thousand.

These are not the kinds of problems that will be solved with conventional wisdom and half-truths; instead, these problems will require the deepest understanding of who we are and how we have arrived at these circumstances. What part of us is still driven by the pure animal we once used to be? What part of us is driven by the new constructions we have been building all around us? What was the original source of humanity's innovative turn, and does that source still continue to work among us? Is there a purpose to what humanity has accomplished over the last one hundred thousand years, and does humanity understand the consequences of what it does now? The value of accurate insights such as Newton's laws and Darwin's evolutionary theory is that they help us navigate an effective path forward, they allow our further actions to be more constructive than destructive, they protect us from floundering about. If we could uncover similar insights regarding human history and human endeavors, then in this area too we might find the means to begin forging a less reckless path, a path that still builds upon the wonders that have become the hallmark features of modern civilization, while leaving the door open to a more hopeful and sustainable future. Thus, there is great potential to be had by attempting to answer these questions. There is great value to be gained by shedding light on the riddle of humanity.

2. Evolution Turned Inside Out

The word used most frequently to explain the human transformation is *evolution*, the implication being that humans must have evolved from pure animals to the rational and innovative creatures they have become today. One form of this idea is the suggestion that evolutionary modernization has been gradually taking place over the entire course of hominin history, for around seven million years, ever since the human branch broke off from the chimps and the great apes. A caricature portrayal of this proposal would be the commonly seen rendering of a procession of increasingly sophisticated hominins, starting with an apelike knuckle-walker, then progressing through a series of more upright and less naked cavemen—each in turn sporting a more advanced weapon or tool—culminating at last in a suit and tie clad businessman holding a briefcase.

Few scientists actually subscribe to such an extreme form of evolutionary gradualism for humans, because there is really nothing in the fossil record to suggest anything modern about hominins until at least the last one million years, and quite possibly until much more recently than that. Nonetheless, scientists still make frequent application of evolutionary theory to help account for humanity's revolutionary turn. For instance, one popular hypothesis is that humans must have acquired something that could be called a language gene at a recent point in their history, giving them the capacity for abstract speech, and because language would confer a selective advantage, the mutation and its resulting behaviors have become thoroughly entrenched within the species. A related suggestion focuses not on language but instead on intelligence, hypothesizing that there must have been genetic mutations targeting human neural capacity, giving rise to brains that can think algorithmically and logically, accounting for the rationality that distinguishes humans from all the other animals. Then there is the field of evolutionary psychology, which takes an even more wide-scale approach to applying evolution to neurology, proposing the existence of many modules within the human brain, each the result of selective adaptations that must have arisen from the survival-and-procreative circumstances of human ancestry.

One other application of evolutionary theory to human history targets not biological change within the species but instead cultural change. The notion of cultural evolution dates back to Darwin's time and has undergone many revisions and comes in a wide variety of flavors, each attempting to explain modern human society within the framework of evolutionary principles. The popularity of cultural evolution gained a boost in the 1970s with the publication of Richard Dawkin's book *The Selfish Gene*, which introduced the concept of a *meme*, a proposed gene-analogous entity that can carry cultural ideas and practices, be replicated and hosted, and compete with other memes for selective advantage.

The desire to apply evolutionary theory to the human transformation is certainly understandable. Evolutionary theory, in combination with genetics, has been extremely successful in describing and explaining the types of changes that species can undergo, and so what could be more promising than applying these concepts to the human transformation, in essence the motherlode of species change. Nonetheless, there are difficulties.

First, the time frame for evolutionary change in modern humans is extremely narrow, since nearly all the impact of the human transformation has occurred within just the last fifty to one hundred thousand years. Significant evolutionary change tends to be much slower and more gradual, more on the order of hundreds of thousands or even millions of years, especially in geological environments that are relatively stable, the condition that exists on Earth in the present age. Lions, gorillas, ants, etc.—most wild species remain much the same today as they were many hundreds of thousands of years ago, and in such circumstances it would be surprising to come across a species undergoing significant evolutionary alteration in an extremely short period of time. This concern about time also applies to cultural evolution, which faces the conundrum of explaining why many modern cultural changes appear to happen almost instantaneously, a characteristic that runs counter to typical evolutionary dynamics.

Second, there is the problem of a lack of specificity. Assume, for instance, a mutation were introduced into the gazelle population that increased leg muscle size and sinew strength. This is a biological change that would create a direct behavioral consequence, namely an increase in running speed, and in turn, this behavioral consequence would directly confer a selective advantage, namely the ability to better survive predator attacks. The chain of events from mutation to evolutionary impact is unbroken—the evolutionary explanation is direct and complete—and this is not uncommon for descriptions of evolutionary change as applied to the plant and animal worlds. In contrast, hypotheses regarding human language genes or human neural mutations fail to provide any element of such a direct connection. The presumption is that the proposed human genetic mutation produces a physical alteration—maybe a change in vocal cords or in synaptic connections—but at the present time these presumed physical alterations remain entirely unspecified. Furthermore, assuming such alterations could be identified, there would then need to be a connection from the physical alteration to the resulting language or intelligence behavior, and given the current state of neuroscience and the like, such direct connection from vocal cords and neurons to specified language and intelligence behaviors seems unlikely to be forthcoming anytime soon. True, such connections might eventually be discovered— science should be allowed some time to work—but until these linkages are revealed, such hypotheses must be considered vague and uncertain as to their correctness.

Finally, there is the problem of applicability. Evolutionary theory and genetics describe *biological* consequences—that is, physical changes in organisms as well as the resulting impact on organisms' observable behavior: a brighter plumage to attract the sexual mate, a louder squawk to ward off the predator, a sharper tooth to subdue the prey. But the distinctive features of the human transformation are not in fact physical or biological, they are instead environmental. There is actually very little in the way of evidence to suggest that *Homo sapiens* has transformed biologically or physically over the last one hundred thousand years—biologically speaking, Cro-Magnon humans appear to be essentially indistinguishable from modern humans—and this is exactly as might be expected for almost any species over such a short period of time. In contrast, there is an overwhelming amount of evidence indicating that the human environment has been transformed dramatically over that exact same period. Compare the African savanna, still very much like the original *Homo sapiens* habitat, with the streets of Manhattan, representative of where many humans live today—you might notice there is a difference.

Of course observable human behavior has also changed dramatically over the last one hundred thousand years, and this changed behavior needs to be accounted for too. But the widespread assumption that there must be something genetic or neurological underlying these new behaviors seems to be overlooking an explanation that is more readily at hand. It is not just changes in biological characteristics that can produce altered organism behaviors, changes in environmental circumstances can *also* produce altered organism behaviors. And in humans, where behaviors have been changing immensely in recent years, it seems downright odd to ascribe such changes to the physical and biological realm, where there is little evidence of any corresponding change at all. It seems more straightforward and parsimonious to attribute such changes to the human environment, which has been transforming just as radically as the behaviors themselves. Think, for instance, of driving behavior. On the African savanna one hundred thousand years ago, *Homo sapiens* would have displayed absolutely no driving behavior at all, and was this because humans were organically incapable of the activity? Today, driving behavior among humans is nearly ubiquitous, and is this because in the intervening years humans have somehow acquired the physical capacity? Why not instead state the more obvious, that humans did not display driving behavior one hundred thousand years ago because there was nothing in the environment to drive, and that humans display driving behavior in abundance today because automobiles have become a foremost feature in the human scene.

If evolutionary theory explains the impact of *biological* characteristics and the behaviors resulting from those characteristics, and if the human transformation is marked by a radical change in *environmental* circumstances and the altered behaviors resulting from those circumstances, then does evolutionary theory even apply to the case of the human transformation? Is this perhaps just a misuse of the tool? Are we stubbornly pounding a square peg into a round hole?

If we fear that the application of evolutionary theory to the human transformation might indeed be a case of pounding a square peg into a round hole, then a corrective course of action would be to modify the shape of the peg. Note that the evolutionary process is defined by a collection of concepts—such as organism, environment, fitness, mutation and selection—and these concepts are described as interacting with one another in the regulative way that defines the process. But is evolution the *only* process that can be defined by these concepts? In other words, can these concepts be rearranged somehow, can they be described as interacting in an alternative way? Is there room here to be a bit more creative, to effectively alter the shape of the peg?

To analyze the evolutionary process and its underlying components in a bit more detail, let us consider a scenario in which the geological environment is essentially stable and mostly isolated—not much unlike the circumstances existing on the Galapagos Islands when the young Darwin visited during the voyage of the *Beagle*. Biological change in such an environment would be essentially driven by two different forms of organism mutation. First, some species, with survival-and-procreative characteristics that fit well to the given environment, will tend to flourish, while other species, with characteristics not so well suited, will tend to disappear. Of course in a stable and isolated environment, this form of change will eventually trend towards an equilibrium, leaving biological change to then happen more frequently by way of the second form of mutation, by way of random genetic variation. And here too, fitness to the environment will determine the likely course of events, with gene mutations that increase an organism's survival-and-procreative chances more likely to gain hold than gene mutations that do not.

From this description—filled with words such as *trend, likely, random* and *chances*—we begin to see the reason why the evolutionary process tends to be more slow and gradual, especially in environments that are relatively stable. The prospect of success for mutations in this scenario, the strength of their fitness, depends not on a targeted certainty but instead on probability. No one mutation, though it indeed be advantaged, is guaranteed particular success—the gazelle with the larger muscle mass and greater sinew strength will indeed be faster, and yet might nonetheless be felled. What is *natural* about natural selection is in large degree this reliance upon random processes and probability; survival of the fittest is primarily a function of the law of large numbers. Thus, the evolutionary process appears to have much in common with the workings of a house-advantaged casino, where with only a few customers playing over just a few nights, the casino might not turn a profit, but given a multitude of customers playing over an abundance of time, the casino is eventually going to thrive.

There are of course other scenarios. For instance, environments are not always stable and isolated, and evolutionary change tends to be more dramatic at times of major environmental shifts—such as after asteroid hits or volcanic eruptions. But in general, the same principles still apply. Whatever environment is given, the organisms within that environment will mutate through survival-and-procreative trials and through genetic variation, with the probabilities underlying natural selection gradually nudging the organisms towards a better environmental fit.

Such descriptions highlighting the evolutionary process and its underlying components are well known and have been highly successful in explicating various cases of biological and species change. So the question to ask now is, does anything about these descriptions correspond to the case of the human transformation? Do the components of the evolutionary process have correlations in the observable features of the human turn? Do we recognize any elements of randomness and chance, is there a heavy reliance upon the law of large numbers? What features of the human transformation might be described as being stable, and what features do we recognize as undergoing sustained mutation? Or to put the entire matter a bit cheekily, if evolutionary theory were the gene, and the human transformation were the surrounding environment, what can we say about the degree of fitness?

Here is what I would propose. The process underlying the human transformation can indeed be described with the exact same components used to describe biological evolution—that is to say, organism, environment, fitness, mutation and selection—but in the description of the human transformation these components take on exchanged roles and operate with one another in entirely different ways, producing an underlying process that in many respects runs *counter* to the evolutionary process, that *opposes* evolution's effects. Thus, the human transformation can be described as not being evolutionary at all, but in fact much more like its opposite. The human transformation is really evolution turned inside out.

First, note that the focus in the case of the human transformation is on just one type of organism—here when we say *organism*, we mean specifically *human* organism and all its differential effects. In evolutionary descriptions, the environment might be taken specifically, but the organisms within that environment are usually considered collectively and much the same. Thus, we can speak of fitness to the environment as a *general* rule and not make exceptions for any kind. We can speak of environments reaching equilibrium without worrying about how one particular species might continuously destroy the balance. The characteristics of biological evolution are therefore operative for every type of organism, whereas the characteristics of the human transformation are privileged to just one species. In the human transformation, no other kind of organism directly takes a role in the ongoing action, no other species has a similar impact as humans do. The human transformation is essentially a one-species show.

Second—and perhaps this is the most important point—take notice of what is stable and what is mutating in the human transformation. In the scenario outlined above depicting biological evolution, it was assumed that it was the environment that was stable, and that the organisms within that environment underwent sustained mutation, through both survival-and-procreative trials and through genetic variation. In the human transformation, however, these roles are reversed. As has been said previously, there is no clearcut evidence and no clearcut reason to assume that humans have changed physically or genetically over say the last one hundred thousand years, any genetic drift could be taken as slight and insignificant. And thus, *Homo sapiens* today is essentially the same as *Homo sapiens* from many years ago—biologically speaking, the organism has remained almost entirely stable. The surrounding environment, on the other hand, well, that is a much different story—the surrounding environment has been anything *but* stable. From fire pits and animal skins and makeshift shelters to electricity and automobiles and towering skyscrapers, humans have been mutating their surroundings in the most massive of ways. There is almost no place left on this entire planet not retouched by human hands, and in the locations where humans typically live, such as in numerous modern cities, nature has been practically expunged from view, replaced everywhere by a relentless reconstruction, a reconstruction targeted always towards human benefit. This fundamental difference between biological evolution and the human transformation cannot be emphasized strongly enough. In biological evolution, the organisms mutate towards the best environment fit; in the human transformation, the environment is being mutated to achieve the best organism fit.

Furthermore, the concepts of fitness and selection, as operative in the human transformation as they are in biological evolution, are nonetheless of an altered nature and produce a much faster paced result. Humans mutate their environment primarily for the purpose of increasing their survival-and-procreative prospects—that is to say, for the purpose of increasing human fitness. Controlled fire, clothing, structured weapons, and all that then follows—nearly every environmental change has been targeted towards improving human robustness. The effectiveness of these endeavors is attested to by the fact that there are now eight billion people living on the planet, and that nearly every square inch of the earth's surface has been made hospitable for humankind. But also take note of this: these environmental mutations, so spectacularly successful for the human species, they have been in no way random. The success of these mutations has not been dependent upon probability. The human transformation is not a consequence of the law of large numbers.

When humans attempt to make an environmental change, they do not put forth a multitude of random variations and then wait to see which one works out the best. What a bizarre approach this would be of making shelters, for instance, trying out hundreds of haphazard architectures and arbitrary materials and then observing which experiments tend to stand up and which experiments tend to fall down; or worse yet, observing which of these shelters' inhabitants better survive and procreate, and which of these shelters' inhabitants tend to disappear. It is not that shelter creation could not be accomplished in this manner, at least in theory—it is after all the tried-and-true method of biological evolution—but arriving at an effective house in this way would take a great deal more time and do considerably less to advance the immediate fitness of this one particular species. Thus, instead of engaging in random trials, humans *target* their environmental mutations and they *anticipate* the results. Humans do not make their selection after the fact, they prejudge their selection at the time of the change. Therefore, selection in the human transformation is not *natural* selection, it is not a child of randomness and not a function of probability. The word we are searching for is *artificial*—artificial selection, artificial construction. *Artificial* is the word that captures the two critical aspects of selection in the human transformation, namely that this selection involves both a restructuring of the given environment as well as an eschewal of any randomness. This is not to say that every human environmental change is successful—indeed a good many are not—but an unsuccessful environmental change is a consequence of an error in judgment, a mistake, it is not an unfortunate spin of a random wheel.

Another characteristic of artificial selection that distinguishes it from its biological counterpart is that artificial selection can be accretive. In the human transformation, most environmental mutations have expanded upon previous mutations, enhancing the original in both breadth and depth. Consider, for instance, the first manmade articles of clothing, and then take a good look at what we wear today. Picture the first tools invented for harvesting crops, and then visit the machines in a modern farmer's shed. Plus environmental mutations can be immediately copied, copied to almost any degree—the effectiveness of one can become the sudden impetus to the effectiveness of thousands, or even millions, of others. And today almost no environmental mutation is complete in and of itself, but instead serves as a link in a hierarchical chain. Look at a house, an airplane, an entire highway system, and then consider all the connective parts of which these artifacts are composed. These accumulative and dependent characteristics stand in sharp contrast with those of natural selection, where nearly every survival-and-procreative trial and nearly every random genetic mutation is essentially an independent event.

Of the observable consequences of this inverted process underlying the human transformation, perhaps none is more striking than its awe-inspiring speed. Not constrained by the lumbering characteristics of biology, not held back by the usually glacial movements of geology, and not delayed by the vicissitudes of random chance, the human transformative process works many orders of magnitude faster than its evolutionary counterpart. This is why there is such a manifest difference in the timescales underlying, on the one hand, biological/evolutionary events, where significant change typically plays out over the course of millions of years, and on the other hand, human events, where significant change has been happening in a mere fraction of that time, and at an accelerating pace.

In summary, the process underlying the human transformation is composed of the very same elements as the process underlying biological evolution, but in the human transformation these elements come together in an entirely different way, producing a new kind of process with a very different impact. It is a process that favors just one type of organism to the exclusion of all the rest. It is a process that exchanges the mutative roles of organism and environment. It is a process in which the selective drive towards fitness disengages from the vagaries of chance, and it is a process that generates accumulative and accelerating change. It is a process that in many respects runs so counter to biological evolution that it can be considered evolution's opposite, even to the degree that it effectively nullifies many of evolution's constraints.

It is perhaps not entirely surprising to think that the process underlying the human transformation would be in some way different from the process underlying biological evolution. Humans are after all clearly unique within the animal kingdom, and to chalk up that uniqueness to only some standard evolutionary processes was always going to seem a little underwhelming, given the immensity of the consequences. We expect that unusual outcomes will be precipitated by unusual causes, and so we anticipate that there will be *something* different behind the human story. But to say that the human transformation runs *counter* to biological evolution, to say that it *opposes* evolution's effects, that claim might take one aback at first, might seem as though it is pushing matters a bit too far. And yet it is this opposition that is the key to understanding much about humanity's unique and current situation, and is particularly crucial for understanding the concept of human freedom.

To see why this is so, we need to take a moment to consider the powerful constraints that biological evolution imposes upon the organisms that fall under its domain. The most obvious constraint is that organisms are almost entirely dependent upon their environmental circumstances, with extremely limited ability to override the given conditions. Having evolved to fit to a particular environment, a species and its organisms will struggle mightily when that environment changes or disappears. Biological history is chock-full of extinctions driven by such environmental transitions—for instance, the dinosaurs, long abundant and long dominant upon this planet, disappeared practically overnight in the dramatically changed circumstances following a massive asteroid hit. Environmental dependency also limits a species' geographical range—sea creatures must live in the sea, forest dwellers must live where there are trees, etc. This is why *Homo sapiens* was limited to certain parts of Africa until around fifty thousand years ago. The species was fit for that particular kind of environment, but not fit for almost any other.

One might wonder at this point why organisms in general do not attempt to alter their surroundings to make their circumstances more suitable to themselves, instead of acquiescing to what the given environment provides. There are examples of tentative movements in this direction: birds reconstruct environmental materials into nests, beavers do the same to construct dams, etc. But these behaviors appear to be the result of evolutionary pressures, and thus once successfully in place, these behaviors do not get generalized, but instead become rigid and attached to the given environment. The problem here is that evolution is the most demanding of taskmasters. The need to survive and procreate becomes so overwhelming for each organism that it effectively hijacks every aspect of the organism's being, leaving essentially no latitude for discovering any alternative approaches. Remember that evolutionary fitness is a function of the law of large numbers, where even the slightest change in probability can lead to a dramatically different long-term outcome, and it would seem that any behavioral effort not acutely focused upon survival and procreation is bound to become a loser in the long-term game. We have noted previously how animal behavior is remarkably similar across species and across time, and this is mostly because all animal behavior shares this laser-like focus upon the need to survive and procreate. This extends so far as to cementing an animal's perceptual characteristics, where environmental features such as food, water, predators, rivals and conspecifics invariably achieve the utmost in foregrounded attention, whereas almost every other aspect of the environment—that is, every aspect not directly concerned with survival and procreation—dissolves into background noise. The background environment does have a great deal of helpful information to offer—as humans have been discovering over the last several thousand years—but for every other species the background environment goes almost entirely unnoticed. An organism striving to survive will keep its eye open for predators, but not for the phases of the moon. An organism feeling the urge to procreate will be keenly attuned to a conspecific partner, but not to the symmetries in the surrounding landscape. Thus, the evolutionary mechanism has the self-perpetuating effect of compelling its participants into a rigid adherence to evolution's rules. Evolution severely limits an organism's perceptual and behavioral freedom.

It is important to recognize at this point that humans too—and not that long ago—were limited in this exact same way. As pure animals, humans were entirely bound by evolution's constraints. Therefore, the most important aspect of the human transformation has been the loosening of these binds, a loosening that could not be achieved by just any random characteristic, but instead by a process directly countering evolution's constrictive effects. The primary mechanism of this loosening has been to turn the mutative formula around, with humans altering their surroundings instead of waiting to be altered themselves. Originally fit just for the African plains, humans have conquered colder climates with the mutative benefits of fire, clothing and shelters; have conquered the expansive seas with the transformative advantages of ships and submarines; have conquered, most outrageously, even the darkness of space and the distant reach of the moon, with the modifying aid of spaceships, helmets and suits. In fact, so successful have humans become at bending their surroundings to their own personal needs, that few today would find themselves at all comfortable left to their own devices on the original African plains.

Furthermore, at the core of these environmental alterations stands a perceptual awareness that has clearly expanded from what humans experienced before, when every ounce of their attention was given strictly to the immediate needs of survival and procreation. Humans do still retain much of this survival-and-procreative awareness—food, drink, sex, rivalries, etc. still garner a great deal of human attention. But humans, unlike every other kind of organism, are no longer *restricted* to these perceptions. Today humans perceive a great deal more about their surrounding environment, they have slowly but surely had their blinders removed. Humans can keep an eye open for predators, and still observe the phases of the moon. Humans can remain keenly attuned to a conspecific partner, and yet be aware of the symmetries in the surrounding landscape. In consequence of this greater perceptual freedom, humans have built up a broader awareness of the pattern, structure and form contained within the spaces around them, and they have made use of this broader awareness to reconstruct so many different aspects of their surrounding world.

None of this yet explains how and why humans first began the process of altering their environment, or how humans first became perceptually aware of the environment's expanded artificial potential—this is a topic that will be taken up in great detail later on. But for now it is enough to recognize that these characteristics of the human transformation work to nullify the constraints of biological evolution. By mutating the environment through artificial reconstruction, by perceiving into the surroundings beyond just evolutionary necessity, humans have gained for themselves an unprecedented level of biological freedom, a freedom with revolutionary and immense consequence. Today humans can *sense* this freedom, they have even given it a name—it is called *free will*. But it is important to understand that free will is not something neurological or psychological or even philosophical. Human freedom is derived from the entirely observable actions of humans reconstructing their environment to their own benefit, and from the entirely observable consequence that humans have largely unshackled themselves from the chains of biological evolution. Unlike every other species, and unlike humans from not that long ago, humans today find themselves no longer evolution bound.

To say that humans were once pure animal implies that the phrase no longer applies. But of course humans are still animal, that part of the terminology must remain intact—humans are born, humans die, humans retain all the usual animal needs and instincts. So in the phrase *pure animal*, it is the word *pure* that must disappear, implying in turn that humans in their modern circumstances are to be described as animal *and* something else. This something else should capture what has been added because of the human transformation, capture what distinguishes modern humans from all the other animals and distinguishes modern humans from their former purely animal selves. Thus, I would propose that modern humans be characterized by the phrase *animal and construct*.

The term *animal* of course requires no further explanation. The term *construct* has been chosen because it has dual effect, capturing the two essential and related aspects of the modern human condition:

1.   The artificial reconstruction of the human environment; and
2.   The novel behaviors resulting from that artificial reconstruction.

What determines the non-animal aspect of humans today is the non-natural setting in which humans live. Ironically, many humans are scarcely aware that they live in an artificial environment—a surrounding of clothes, houses, schools, cars and so on seems entirely "natural," having been the default for almost every person from birth. But in fact there is almost nothing of nature left in the human environment—literally everywhere one looks one sees instead artificial reconstruction. To get a sense of just how enormous and just how widespread this alteration has become, consider the North American continent and what it must have looked like just a few hundred years ago, when the human impact was still minimal, the land a nearly untouched natural splendor—mountains, prairies, swamps, woodlands, rivers, streams, nature in its most pristine abundance. Now take a good look at what the North American continent has become today. All across its vast area we now find a blanketing cornucopia of artifacts: roads, houses, towers, wires, pipes, fences, shopping malls, office complexes, airports, bridges, tunnels—the catalog of construction goes on and on. Plus think of all the large cities, where almost nothing remains of what stood there before. And it is not just the expansiveness of all this change, it is also its detail and depth. Think of just one apartment building, then think of just one floor in that building, then think of just one room on that one floor, and then count all the room's artificial contents: television, carpeting, air conditioner, furniture, utensils, pictures, books, computers—once again, the catalog of construction goes on and on. We humans live in an ocean of artificiality, we find it "natural" only because we are so thoroughly drenched in its ubiquitous effect.

As extensive as all this environmental construction has become, perhaps even more pervasive are the behavioral changes this construction has provoked. Every environmental mutation prompts a human behavioral consequence. Controlled fire impacts the way humans prepare and eat food, clothing changes the range of human movement, etc. Indeed it is something of an ongoing cycle—an environmental change prompts a behavioral change, which in turn provides the means for further environmental change, and thus the mutations, both environmental and behavioral, accumulate. Today the enormous catalog of artificiality in the human environment is matched by an equally immense catalog of newfound and unnatural behaviors: cooking, driving, reading, writing, calculating, showering, shaving, voting, changing channels, changing clothes, playing video games—once again, the list goes on and on. And every one of these newfound human behaviors can be traced back to some new artifact introduced into the human environment, something that did not exist there before. We drive because there are cars on the street, we read because there are books on the shelf, we shave because there are razors in the cabinet. Thus, we see how the word *construct* and its two related components—the reconstruction of the human environment, and the behaviors those reconstructions engender—this captures exactly the amount of change that has been layered on to humanity over the course of the human transformation. For if we were to remove every artificial feature that now exists in the human environment, and if we were to suppress every human behavior that can trace its origin back to those removed artifacts, then all that would then remain would be our biological and evolutionary selves, all that would then remain would be the pure animal that *Homo sapiens* once was.

Finally, it should be noted that the circumstance of humans as both animal and construct creates something of a paradoxical conflict—these two aspects of modern humanity do not always play so well together. The animal aspect of humanity has the insistent effect of tugging humans backwards in time, towards an era of more restrictive biological need and of temporal and spatial immediacy. Humans today still experience the pressing urges of food, sex, dominance and safety, betraying the species' survival-and-procreative underpinnings, and we may not fully recognize how much of our modern living has been slyly arranged to serve as an outlet for these evolutionary demands. Hunting, org charts, sports rivalries, beauty pageants—tear away all the sublimation and what remains are ardent attempts to scratch the itch of an unquenched animal need. Thoreau understood that need, having famously included a passage in *Walden* about happening upon a woodchuck on the path and wanting to seize the creature in his hands and devour it raw. There is nothing surprising or maladjusted about any of these desires, actions and behaviors, they are the inevitable consequence of humans still retaining all the characteristics of a biological organism.

At the same time, the constructive aspect of humanity propels humans in the opposite direction, towards expanding innovation and towards a broader temporal and spatial awareness. Environmental reconstruction does require diligent and persistent effort, but the long-term rewards of that effort have now become apparent to almost everyone—a greater satisfaction of needs, abundant physical comforts, a counterweight against boredom, and a sense of forward purpose. Plus we should not forget the most *fundamental* reward that human construction bestows, namely a much greater degree of human freedom. The most challenging obstacle on this path towards human progress appears to be the overcoming of rudimentary instinct. To expand their horizons beyond just the here and now, humans must build up the discipline to postpone their immediate needs, must find the strength to delay their gratifications. Abstinence, austerity, rigor, sobriety, monasticism, willpower—so many different forms of asceticism, all targeted to suppressing the beast within. These strivings are, in the most fundamental sense, entirely unnatural, but for all that they are in no way to be derided. Human progress appears to be a noble quest, a swimming against the entropic tide, an endeavor to build an actual paradise here on the planet Earth.

This inner human conflict between animal and construct is both challenging and relentless, and it is a conflict that has been growing ever more intense since the first days of the human turn. But this is a conflict that is unavoidable for a species that has been fashioned by two entirely different processes, processes that work to oppose each other and that run in counter directions. It is the inevitable consequence of a species originally forged in the long-running furnace of biological evolution, and now so lately and so thoroughly reshaped by a process that works to defy all of evolution's effects.

3. The Construction of Intelligence

Understanding that artificial reconstruction of the human environment serves as a fundamental component of the human transformation does bring us one step closer to identifying a cause for this uniquely human occurrence. We can now recognize that humans have somehow gained a broader perceptual awareness of their surrounding environment, an awareness that has allowed the species to break free from a strictly survival-and-procreative focus, and this broader perceptual awareness, centered around the concepts of artificial pattern, structure and form, has helped spark an effective reshaping of the human environment and a radical expansion of human behavior. So we are nearly prepared to ask, what characteristic, what element within the human population, could be the key that has unlocked this broader perceptual awareness?

We will explore that question in great detail shortly, but for now I must ask your indulgence to postpone that discussion for a bit longer. The purpose of the delay is to take some time to examine in greater depth the activity of human environmental construction. As it happens, we can approach this topic from an entirely different angle and can view it in a completely different light, one that has modern scientific consequence. This additional analysis will prove to be fruitful. It will provide greater information about what is the most basic human quality that lies at the core of the human transformation, and furthermore, this analysis will help solve a conundrum that has been puzzling scientists for the last thirty-five years.

As a reminder, in characterizing modern humans as both animal and construct, the word *construct* was used to denote two separate but related characteristics:

1. The artificial reconstruction of the human environment; and
2. The novel behaviors resulting from that artificial reconstruction.

What I am going to propose now is that there is *another* word, besides *construct*, that can be used to capture the combination of these two related characteristics, a word that is in widespread use and that is clearly foundational to what makes humans unique. That other word is *intelligence*.

Although it might seem at first that I am employing the word *intelligence* in a somewhat different sense than that of the typical connotation, rest assured that there is nothing arbitrary about my proposal. In the discussion that follows, I will directly connect human environmental construction to the basic tool for measuring human intelligence, the IQ exam, and I will go on to demonstrate that performance on an IQ exam not only assesses the traits we commonly associate with intelligence, but also, and quite equivalently, assesses our interaction with the artificial and constructed material of the human world. This demonstration will directly link measurable human intelligence to the observable features of the human transformation, and thus will mark intelligence as the most fundamental human quality underlying that transformation (as opposed, for instance, to say language ability or collective learning). But this demonstration will also necessitate a reassessment of the word *intelligence*, requiring that intelligence be understood more broadly than as just a neurological phenomenon. We will see that to arrive at a complete understanding of intelligence, to provide a cogent explanation for the observed patterns of intelligence scores, we must incorporate into our definition of intelligence an adequate provision for the totality of constructed artifacts existing within the human environment, the material out of which intelligence is ultimately constructed.

And there will be a bonus.

During the twentieth century, it was discovered that each successive generation was scoring progressively better on intelligence exams. In other words, raw intelligence scores were consistently and significantly increasing over time. This increase in performance was large enough that it required intelligence exams to be modified on a frequent basis, typically towards greater complexity and difficulty. Several researchers had noticed this phenomenon, but it was James Flynn in the 1980s who provided abundant evidence that the phenomenon was essentially universal, thereby drawing greater attention to it, and the phenomenon would be eventually dubbed the Flynn effect. Over the past several decades there have been many attempts to explain the Flynn effect—increasing genetic robustness, better nutrition, expanded education, abstruse theories about fast and slow life, etc.—but none of these suggestions have proven to be compelling, and thus the Flynn effect has continued to remain a scientific mystery.

But as it happens, our subject from the previous section—the non-evolutionary and artificial environmental reconstruction that lies at the core of recent human history—this turns out to have great relevance to the phenomenon of an increasing human intelligence. By linking the contents of an IQ exam to the observable features of the human transformation, and by exploring the potential for human intelligence performance throughout the course of human history, we will come to realize that an increase in human intelligence is not just a twentieth-century aberration but is indeed a fundamental property of the human transformation itself. That is, the Flynn effect has been accompanying humanity ever since the beginning of the human turn, with the corresponding increase in human intelligence directly tied to the amount of artificial construction that has been accruing in the human environment, thus yielding an extremely straightforward and elegant explanation of the Flynn effect.

Intelligence is one of those words that does not seem to have a completely agreed-upon definition. There are several characteristics commonly associated with intelligence—reasoning ability, problem solving, capacity to learn, creativity, etc.—but none of these characteristics, singularly or in combination, quite manages to capture everything that is meant by the word *intelligence*. There appears to be a certain *je ne sais quoi* element to intelligence—we can easily recognize smartness when we see it and experience it, but we seem to have a hard time putting a finger on exactly what it is.

Scientists sidestep this difficulty by sticking to what they can measure. The scientific approach to intelligence focuses both on the basic tool for assessing intelligence, the IQ exam, as well as on the statistical analyses that can be obtained from IQ exam performance. These quantitative efforts have been historically productive. The first IQ tests were developed around the year 1900, and throughout the following century, researchers kept themselves busy putting IQ scores through a series of statistical investigations, teasing out much of what is currently understood about human intelligence. One of the earliest and most basic results from these efforts came in the use of factor analysis to arrive at a *general* factor for intelligence, typically quantified in a statistic known as Spearman's *g* (named after Charles Spearman, its originator). In short, Spearman's *g* captures the notion of a general intelligence ability, one that shows up in the correlation of performance across different types of intelligence tasks—that is, a person who can score well on one type of intelligence test will typically also score well on the others. Furthermore, IQ exam analysis in combination with identical twin and other family-based studies, has shown that one's general intelligence ability is influenced in large degree by one's genetic makeup—more so than, for instance, one's upbringing or environment—thus pointing to a significant biological/neurological component underlying individual intelligence differences.

These exam-driven conclusions famously prompted psychologist Edwin Boring in 1923 to define intelligence as the thing that gets measured by intelligence tests. Boring partly intended his aphorism as a warning, noting the extremely insular nature of many intelligence statistics. But he also seemed to suggest that in a certain sense his seemingly tautological definition was capturing a meaningful truth, one that could be built upon if approached in the right way. In my opinion, Boring's definition actually turns out to be both valid and quite good, that defining intelligence by linking it to intelligence exams actually has a large degree of substantive merit. I say this for two reasons, one of which is widely known, and the other of which seems to have been given hardly any attention at all.

The widely known reason is this. Although it is indeed tautological to say that intelligence is what gets measured by intelligence tests, it has also been repeatedly demonstrated that intelligence tests have a significance that goes beyond that which they measure. This is because performance on intelligence exams has been shown to be highly correlated with many aspects of human life, aspects that have great importance to people navigating their way through the human world. Academic success, career prospects, socioeconomic circumstances, even health and longevity—all these areas correlate significantly to IQ exam performance, with better IQ exam performance pointing towards cheerier prospects in actual life. So whatever quality it is that is being measured by an IQ exam—call it intelligence if you will—it tends to translate to happier prospects outside the exam room, meaning that intelligence statistics serve more than just an inward-looking purpose.

The less well-known reason centers around the question of what exactly is it about any particular test—that is, what observable features must that test have—in order for it to qualify as an *intelligence* test. Consider these two possibilities. In the first instance, I write down a dozen or so math and logic problems on a sheet of paper, give the paper to a subject to fill out, and then afterwards sum up the correct answers. In the second instance, I give the subject a sheet of paper and ask him or her to crumple it up and throw it as far as he or she can, and then afterwards I measure the distance the paper traveled. Nearly everyone would agree that the first instance could qualify as an intelligence test, and that the second instance would not. But why? Both examples are a test of human ability and both provide a numerical measure that can be compared, so why is one considered appropriate for assessing intelligence and the other one is not?

One way of answering this question might be to note that performance on the first test will likely have some correlation with other intelligence tests, and that the second test is unlikely to have such a correlation. But this just gets us back into tautology land, where a test's acceptance into the intelligence test club is done solely by reference to tests that have already been accepted. This is not really what we are after. What we would like to be able to do is to identify a test as an intelligence test by something other than saying that it is used for measuring intelligence. In other words, if all intelligence tests were to be described simply as perceived artifacts, without reference to what purpose they serve, would there be a characteristic or characteristics they all would have in common?

This question prompts an investigation into the *contents* of an intelligence exam, which in my estimation is the most important thing *about* an intelligence exam, even if the topic seems to have been given very little attention in the literature. To understand why it is that an IQ exam succeeds in measuring intelligence, we need to better understand what it is that an IQ exam is composed of. This investigation also has a historical component to it. If we were to contemplate the possibility of intelligence exams having been available throughout human history, would the contents of those exams have remained static over time, or would they have needed to be altered? This is where the investigation connects to the broader topic we have already been discussing, for as we shall see, the contents of an intelligence exam cannot be arbitrary, but instead must have a particular characteristic to them, a characteristic intimately connected to the fundamental features of the human transformation.

Some of the earliest IQ exams to gain acceptance and application were the Stanford-Binet and Wechsler scales, tests that are still in widespread use today. The contents of these particular tests cover a broad range of subjects, including vocabulary, arithmetic, number-letter sequencing, general knowledge, similarities, visual-spatial puzzles, and so on. The popularity of these exams has of course influenced what is considered to be the standard content for intelligence tests, but it should also be noted that there are many alternatives available. For instance, Raven's Progressive Matrices, a test composed of a logical series of spatial/temporal patterns, has been shown to be effective in assessing non-verbal intelligence, and has been one of the tests displaying the greatest amount of Flynn effect over the past century. Indeed, there are essentially an endless number of tasks that could be successfully employed, at least to some degree, to assess various aspects of intelligence, everything from multiplication tables to chess problems to driver's license exams. So what is it about the contents of all these tests and tasks that connect them to the subject of intelligence, what could be their common thread?

One approach to discovering the type of content that an intelligence exam must have would be to consider first those tests that are clearly *not* acceptable for assessing intelligence. Much like the example of throwing the crumpled-up sheet of paper, tests that measure for qualities such as running speed, strength, visual acuity, agility, fertility and so on would not be acceptable as measures of intelligence, despite the fact these qualities are often important to humans in their everyday lives. The contents of such tests have a particular nature that would appear to disqualify them—namely, these tests are composed primarily of activities that are athletic, physical, biological, and we seem to intuitively understand that these particular abilities and activities are exactly the ones that need to be *excluded* when assessing intelligence. This intuition has a rational basis. When we examine the types of tests that are being ruled out here, and when we consider the activities and abilities that underlie them, we recognize that we could actually administer such tests—albeit with some difficulty—even to wild animals, and we also could have administered such tests to humans back when they were in the state of being pure animals themselves. The contents of such tests have an evolutionary/biological basis, they are intimately connected with survival-and-procreative fitness. Thus, they measure the *animal* aspect of humankind, and they do not measure the aspect that has been added to humanity in the more recent years.

And this gets us to the common thread underlying intelligence tests and tasks.

When we examine the contents of any intelligence test, the one word that should immediately strike us is *artificial*. Artificial patterns, artificial structures, artificial form. Intelligence tests are composed of artificial constructions—words, digits, sequences, puzzles, matrices, etc.—and when we score an individual's performance on an intelligence test, what we are assessing is that person's ability to understand and to manipulate these artificial constructions. And since *all* intelligence tasks are composed of artificial constructions, it should come as no surprise that performance across these tasks tends to correlate, with one's general intelligence ability essentially being a measure of one's overall effectiveness at manipulating artificial construction at large.

But artificial construction at large is exactly the defining observable feature of the human transformation, and human *responsiveness* to artificial construction is the telltale behavior distinguishing humans from all the other animals. The originators of the first intelligence tests may not have realized it, but what they were building were assessments of human modernity, assessments of human capacity for the non-natural and constructed artifacts that have been accruing in the surroundings ever since the beginning of the human turn. The artificial pattern, structure and form to be found on every intelligence test mirrors the artificial pattern, structure and form to be found in the human environment, and thus the contents of an intelligence test serve as a *proxy* for the type of artificial complexity that needs to be navigated by humans in their everyday lives. And so here too, it should come as no surprise that performance on these proxies correlates significantly to successful prospects in the everyday world, because for most humans today, effective navigation and manipulation of the environment's artificial features is often more important and more consequential than effective navigation in the biological/evolutionary realm.

A further approach to exploring IQ exam contents and their relationship to the artificial reconstruction of the human environment—that is to say, to the human transformation itself—would be to contemplate IQ exam performance over the entire course of human history. Of course since the first intelligence tests were not created until around the year 1900, we do not have explicit data from before that time, neither on what characteristics intelligence exams might have possessed during those earlier years, nor on the level of performance such exams might have evoked. Therefore, we will need to resort to some imagination. But even with this limitation, it will take very little in the way of effort and reasoning to convince us that intelligence exams from those earlier times would have had to be crafted much differently than they are today, and that intelligence performance throughout those earlier years would have been much diminished from what can be observed in the general population now.

To give some visualization to the investigation, we can assume that scientists have developed a means of time travel that allows them to go back to earlier points in human history for the purpose of administering intelligence tests. We can begin by going back around five thousand years, to the agrarian villages that would soon coalesce into the Mesopotamian civilization. Our time-traveling scientists will have brought with them the current iteration of the Stanford-Binet and Wechsler scales, with the hope of administering translated versions of these tests to the agrarian population. But of course the scientists will quickly encounter some major challenges. In the first place, there is no hope of administering a written version of these tests—five thousand years ago, writing was still on the verge of being invented—and so any intelligence task would have to be delivered orally, making many portions of modern IQ exams essentially impossible to administer. But the problem goes beyond just this. For instance, much of the vocabulary being tested would have to be adjusted, because a large portion of the vocabulary showing up on modern exams represents objects and concepts that have only come into existence after Mesopotamian times. Arithmetic too would have to be essentially removed, since numeracy beyond perhaps counting up to one-two-three was not yet widely practiced. Even something like Raven's Progressive Matrices, a non-verbal exam with geometric patterns that could be drawn perhaps on tree bark—or in the dirt, for that matter—would still cause problems for this particular population. Having been raised in a world without the regularity of clocks, street grids, etc., the Mesopotamians would likely find the rigidly structured patterns of the Raven's questions to be far outside their ken, with few having even an inkling of what was being asked of them.

Thus, the scientists will soon find they need to abandon their efforts at administering any modern IQ exams they may have brought with them, and might even be wondering if Mesopotamian performance on such exams should be essentially marked near zero. But these scientists want to obtain an accurate and observed measure of the overall level of intelligence for this population, and also to assess whether there are any intelligence differences *within* the population, so the scientists scramble together an alternative test, a spoken and drawn exam composed out of tasks that the Mesopotamians can more easily relate to and understand. The vocabulary problems end up being more basic than what is found on modern tests, but at least a majority of the Mesopotamian test takers can effectively respond. The mathematical and geometrical questions will also seem crude by modern standards, but at least they now correspond to what Mesopotamians encounter in their everyday lives. More questions can be composed out of the basic structural features arising from such activities as simple farming, irrigation, pottery making and so on. The resulting test might seem quite simple to the scientists—one of them might even remark, "Almost everyone from our era would score nearly one hundred percent"—but when administered to the Mesopotamians, a familiar range of outcomes does emerge, confirming that these scientists have done an admirable job at putting together their makeshift exam. Some Mesopotamians score well, some score poorly, and most score somewhere in the middle. "Well, at least the *curve* looks familiar," one of the scientists remarks. The scientists might then leave these Mesopotamian times with a vague sense of puzzlement over what all these results could mean, but at least they have acquired some substantive data, and can continue onwards with their historical quest.

The next temporal destination goes back to around twenty-five thousand years ago, before the time of agriculture and villages but after the out-of-Africa migration. These humans are still universally hunter-gatherers, but they are not without some modern accompaniments: crafted weapons, clothing, fire pits, ornamental jewelry, cave paintings. Our scientists know better this time than to bother with the Stanford-Binet and Wechsler scales, but their first thought is to offer the makeshift exam they had crafted for the Mesopotamians to this new population, to see if that exam could still coax out some meaningful results. However, this turns out to be mostly not the case, and this is because much of what the scientists had developed for the Mesopotamians was forged out of the agrarian concepts and abilities that had only been introduced into human experience sometime just before the Mesopotamian era, and thus would be utterly unfamiliar for these hunter-gatherer tribes. So once again our resourceful scientists patch together a different kind of test, one with tasks more familiar for their nomadic subjects. Out of necessity, the vocabulary is now even more limited than what was applied to the Mesopotamians, and the numeracy and geometric questions end up seeming almost toddler-like. Other questions are composed out of the underlying skills the scientists can glean from observed practices of fire making, weapon construction, animal rendering, and simple cooking. Indeed, so naturalistic and primitive would appear to be the lives of these hunter-gatherers that one of the scientists asks if they should not instead be testing for such skills as speed, strength and sexual dominance, until the other scientists object that these are not the kinds of skills one typically associates with intelligence. So the scientists stick with the basic exam they can manage to form out of the material at hand, and once again they find their efforts rewarded with a familiar set of results. Some of the hunter-gatherers score well on the new exam, some score poorly, and most score somewhere in the middle, demonstrating that for this population too there is an observable degree of intelligence capacity, with the capacity differing in the normal way from person to person.

Finally, the scientists travel back to a few hundred thousand years ago, when humans had not yet begun to reconstruct their environment, when the surroundings remained entirely natural and humans were still essentially living the lives of pure animals. The scientists quickly realize, with regard to intelligence testing, that there is really nothing they can do. It is not just that the modern exams like Stanford-Binet and Wechsler cannot be applied, and it is not just that the exams developed for the Mesopotamians and previous hunter-gatherers cannot be administered as well, it is that these scientists cannot even craft a new kind of test, one more accessible to this ancient population. This is because there is nothing out of which a new test can be composed—no abstract language, no mathematics, no crafted weaponry, no clothing, no cooking. There is not a single artificial feature to be found in this environment, and there is not a single human behavior that cannot be described as being animal-like. The only abilities these scientists could possibly test for and measure would be the kinds of abilities that could just as easily be found in almost any other type of creature, abilities that are entirely physical and biological, abilities directly concerned with survival and procreation. Thus, the scientists conclude that there is no intelligence to be found or measured in this population—at least no intelligence beyond that which could be attributed to *any* animal population.

But the scientists no sooner arrive at this conclusion than they begin to have some second thoughts. After all, the hunter-gatherers they had just previously visited, from twenty-five thousand years ago, did display some measurable intelligence capacity, and furthermore these ancient humans now standing before them, from a few hundred thousand years ago, do not appear to be, physically or genetically, all that much different from the previously visited populations—biologically speaking, all the visited humans have appeared to be essentially the same. So why did the previous hunter-gatherers display some level of intelligence, while this more ancient group seems to be displaying none at all? For that matter, why have *any* of the visited populations displayed a different level of intelligence from the others, or from modern norms?

"You know what I wish we could do," says one of the scientists. "I wish we could take one of these newborns from this ancient population back with us to modern times, and then raise him there. What I would like to know is this: would he still display no intelligence at all, or as he grew up in the modern world would he begin to demonstrate a level of intelligence similar to other modern humans?" The scientists begin to think about this question, and they end up thinking about it for a very long time.

The conundrum of the scientist's question is this. On the one hand, if intelligence is just a neural ability, then these ancient humans from a few hundred thousand years ago, because they are demonstrating no measurable level of intelligence, must be entirely lacking in this neural ability. Therefore, an ancient newborn snatched from his ancient times and raised instead in the modern era, because he lacks the neural ability, would continue to display no signs of intelligence. Furthermore, this neural ability must have somehow been introduced into the human population by the time of the hunter-gatherers of twenty-five thousand years ago, because that population was capable of taking an intelligence test—simple though it may have been—and of displaying a measurable level of intelligence. Also, this neural ability must have significantly increased by the time of the Mesopotamians, who were capable of taking a more complex intelligence exam, and thereby demonstrating a greater level of measurable intelligence. And finally, this neural ability must have increased by orders of magnitude yet once more by the time of modern humans, who find themselves perfectly capable of handling the complexities of Stanford-Binet and Wechsler.

But on the other hand, such an enormous increase in neural ability would appear to defy almost every known biological and evolutionary principle. There is no other human biological ability that has undergone similar transformation in such a short period of time, and under normal circumstances, there would be no reason to expect such a large-scale, species-wide and progressive neural change. Biologically speaking, the humans from two hundred thousand years ago should be essentially the same as the humans of today, and although it has now become commonplace to say that our human brains have somehow become smarter over that interval of time—that is to say, physically more effective—if we were to be biologically honest with ourselves and were to detail the type and degree of neural alteration we are actually contemplating, then we would have to admit we are engaging in a scarcely plausible biological leap of faith.

And yet still…. If physical neural ability has not been changing in *Homo sapiens*, then what else could be driving the human intelligence differences that are apparent across the entire course of human history? It appears to be a conundrum.

Here would be my proposal. If we were to spend enough time thinking about the scientist's question, we might eventually come to realize that we have every reason to expect that a newborn snatched from an ancient human population and raised instead in the modern era would actually achieve a level of intelligence commensurate with that of his modernly born peers. Furthermore, if that same newborn were instead to be raised among the hunter-gatherers from twenty-five thousand years ago, he would achieve a corresponding level of hunter-gatherer intelligence, and likewise if that newborn were to be raised among the Mesopotamians he would achieve a Mesopotamian level of intelligence. This newborn, along with his fellow humans from a few hundred thousand years ago, does not lack for intellectual ability—biologically speaking, he should possess the same neural capacity as do other sapiens, including modern humans. What he and his fellow ancient humans lack is any artificial complexity in their surrounding environment towards which they can *apply* their intellectual capacity. Human intelligence is not simply a neural ability, human intelligence is far more comprehensive than that. Human intelligence is better described as the effective manipulation and navigation of the artificial construction to be found in the human environment, a skill that requires both the neural ability and *also* the environment towards which that neural ability can be applied. Thus, note the resulting consequence: no artificial construction in the environment translates to no measurable intelligence.

Furthermore, an *increase* in artificial construction translates to an *increase* in measurable intelligence. The quantity of artificial construction to be found in the hunter-gatherer environment of twenty-five thousand years ago was not zero, was not nonexistent, but on the other hand it was still quite small by modern standards, both in total amount and in depth of complexity. Any intelligence exam that would be appropriate and useful for that particular population would have to reflect this limited quantity of artificial construction. A modern exam such as Stanford-Binet or Wechsler would be too complex and would contain too many features with which these hunter-gatherers would be unfamiliar, and thus would not serve as a useful proxy for hunter-gatherer intelligence. In comparable fashion, the quantity of artificial construction to be found in the agrarian Mesopotamian environment of about five thousand years ago was greater than that to be found in the hunter-gatherer environment, and yet still much less than that to be found in modern settings. Therefore, any intelligence exam intended for the Mesopotamians would need to be calibrated to reflect their particular quantity and type of artificial environmental construction. Stanford-Binet and Wechsler would still be too complex and unfamiliar, and thus would likely overwhelm the Mesopotamians, while at the same time the exam constructed for the hunter-gatherer population would not be challenging enough, leading to mostly excellent scores for nearly every Mesopotamian, so much so that individual intelligence differences could not emerge. Finally, humans of the early twenty-first century, having been raised in an environment overflowing with buildings, roadways, televisions, computers and countless other complex artifacts, and having from a young age developed a broad vocabulary consistent with the broadness of their world, and having studied algebra and configured their phones and so on, would not find themselves challenged by exams constructed for the Mesopotamians and hunter-gatherers. Modern humans require an exam with greater complexity and greater variety in order to demonstrate their impressively broad skills at navigating the complex features of their modern world.

Of course all this has a direct connection to the Flynn effect. Intelligence exams with contents that contain greater complexity and greater variety are palpable indicators of an increased level of overall intelligence. And thus, we can conclude that measurable human intelligence has been increasing throughout human history, ever since the beginning of the human transformation, an increase that would have been reflected in the increasing complexity and difficulty of intelligence exams, had such exams been available to earlier populations. Furthermore, this increase in measurable intelligence is directly attributable to the fact that humans have been forced to navigate an increasing amount of artificial complexity in their surrounding world. This means that the accruing amount of artificial environmental construction arising from the human transformation serves as the sole driver and the sole explanation of the Flynn effect.

Note that although our time-traveling illustration does require some imaginative reasoning, this reasoning remains entirely consistent with what has actually taken place over the past century, with respect to actual intelligence performance on actual intelligence exams. Over the past one hundred years or so, ever since the invention of IQ tests, each generation has scored better and better as the tests have aged, so much so that individual intelligence differences begin to disappear, rendering older exams essentially obsolete. Intelligence researchers have realized that they need to frequently modify their exams, adding new types of material and making the questions generally more complex and difficult. These researchers may be somewhat puzzled as to what could be driving these changes, but as our historical analysis has indicated, these researchers have not been witnessing just a twentieth-century fluke. This increase in overall human intelligence, now dubbed the Flynn effect, has been shadowing human existence ever since the beginning of the human turn, and what these researchers have been witnessing is just the modern continuation of an extremely long-running phenomenon.

And from the historical perspective, there really should be nothing surprising about this phenomenon. If humans were indeed once pure animals, then it is perfectly reasonable to say that humans at that time displayed no intelligence at all, at least no intelligence beyond that which could be attributed to any animal species. And since humans today clearly do possess an observable and measurable level of intelligence, then over the course of human history, measurable human intelligence has increased from absolute zero to a substantive number, and *by definition* that increase is a Flynn effect. The only question is whether that change has been sudden or gradual, but any reasonable reflection on the events of the human transformation will make it more than clear that the change cannot have been sudden, but that the increase in human intelligence has been progressing steadily throughout human history, an increase driven by the accruing amount of artificial construction contained within the human environment.

What I will attempt to do now is to build a quantified scenario that incorporates the concepts and assumptions from the above discussion. The purpose of this scenario is to demonstrate the pattern of IQ scores that emerges when we take into account artificial environmental construction when developing, administering and scoring IQ exams. The pattern of IQ scores emerging from this scenario will be exactly the same pattern that has been observed on actual intelligence tests over the past one hundred years, and this pattern will consist of both a stable level of general intelligence ability (such as that quantified by Spearman's *g*) as well as an increase in overall measured intelligence (that is to say, a Flynn effect). The scenario itself will make clear that there is nothing contradictory about these two results. A stable general intelligence ability is perfectly consistent with an increase in overall measured intelligence, as long as our definition of intelligence incorporates the impact of the total amount of artificial construction contained within the human environment.

The scenario to be constructed arises from the following assumptions and stipulations:

1. We assume we can investigate the intelligence characteristics at four sequential points in time, call them Time 0, Time 1, Time 2, and Time 3. These points in time are of course arbitrary, marked out solely for the purpose of the demonstration, but if it helps to visualize them, we can think of Time 0 as being a few hundred thousand years ago, when humans were still pure animals, Time 1 as being around twenty-five thousand years ago, the era of efficient hunter-gatherers, Time 2 as being around five thousand years ago, the agrarian dawn of the Mesopotamian civilization, and Time 3 as being now, early in the twenty-first century. Do keep in mind, however, that this is just for visualization—the demonstration remains essentially the same for any four sequential points in time, as long as the interval between them allows for at least a new generation or two.

2. We assume we can measure and quantify the amount of artificial construction in the human environment at each point in time. Furthermore, we assume, consistent with human history, that the amount of artificial construction increases with time. For this particular scenario, we will stipulate that the quantified amount of artificial construction measured at Time 0 is 0, that the amount of artificial construction at Time 1 is 10, that the amount of artificial construction at Time 2 is 20, and that the amount of artificial construction at Time 3 is 100. Per the visualization, this would be the equivalent of saying that there was no artificial construction in the human environment a few hundred thousand years ago, that there was a quantified level of artificial construction measuring 10 for the hunter-gatherers (a reflection of fire pits, simple cooking, ornamental jewelry, etc.), that there was a quantified level of artificial construction measuring 20 for the Mesopotamians (a reflection of simple abodes, irrigation techniques, pottery making, etc.), and that there is a quantified level of artificial construction measuring 100 in the early twenty-first century (reflecting highways, computers, skyscrapers, etc.). This scale likely shortchanges the modern era, but it still serves well for illustrative purposes.

3. We assume that at Times 1, 2 and 3, we can construct and administer a battery of IQ tests for the population of that era. Furthermore, we assume that each of these batteries of tests is an equally accurate proxy for the amount and type of artificial construction contained within the environment of that time. Thus, the IQ tests of Time 1 have contents that reflect the measured level of 10 for artificial construction at Time 1, the IQ tests of Time 2 have contents that reflect the measured level of 20 for artificial construction at Time 2, and the IQ tests of Time 3 have contents that reflect the measured level of 100 for artificial construction at Time 3. In practice, this means that the tests become more varied and more complex as time goes on, just as was described for the hunter-gatherers, Mesopotamians, etc., and just as has been observed on actual intelligence tests over the past one hundred years.

4. Since the measured level of artificial construction at Time 0 is stipulated to be 0, we further stipulate that no IQ test can be constructed and administered to this population.

5. Since the battery of IQ tests at each point in time is assumed to be an equally accurate proxy for that era's artificial environmental construction, we further assume that each population will score similarly on its particular set of exams. Consistent with this assumption, we stipulate that each population's results can be demonstrated through the scores of three representative test takers. First, there is Test-taker Low, who answers 50% of the test questions correctly, which turns out to be one standard deviation below the population mean. Next, there is Test-taker Middle, who answers 60% of the test questions correctly, which comes in right at the population mean. And finally, there is Test-taker High, who answers 70% of the test questions correctly, which is one standard deviation above the population mean. We further stipulate that these same levels of representative test-taking ability are in effect at Time 0, even though there is no exam to administer to the Time 0 population.

With these assumptions and stipulations in place, we can now work out what would unfold over the course of this scenario, and what pattern of IQ scores would emerge from these four populations.

There is not much to say about the Time 0 population. With no artificial construction in the environment and no IQ exam to administer, all intelligence scores would have to be marked as zero, and this despite the fact we have stipulated that this population does possess an intelligence capacity similar to that of the other populations. But in this particular environment, there is nothing towards which this population can *apply* its intelligence ability. We are in the realm of pure animals and of no artificial environmental construction, and thus we are also in the realm of no measurable intelligence.

At Time 1, the Time 1 battery of IQ tests is administered to the population, and afterwards the results are normed by determining the statistical mean and standard deviation, the same as is done with real-world exams. With this accomplished, intelligence researchers can then perform many population analyses, since relative performance is all that is needed for this type of research. General intelligence statistics can be gathered, correlations with life outcomes can be scrutinized, and family studies can be conducted showing the extent to which individual general intelligence abilities are genetically determined. Relative and normed IQ performance within a population is the backbone of nearly all intelligence research, and thus this type of research can be readily accomplished with the Time 1 population.

But also at Time 1, an alternative type of statistic can be determined, one that has not been attempted in modern studies. Because this scenario has included the measurement and quantification of the amount of artificial construction in the Time 1 environment, and because the scenario has assumed that the Time 1 battery of IQ tests reflects this level of artificial construction, this information can be used to go beyond just working with relative IQ performance, and can be used to determine an *absolute* intelligence score for each member of this population. It works like this. Test-taker Low answered 50% of the test questions correctly. Since the contents of the Time 1 tests reflect an amount of 10 for artificial construction in the Time 1 environment, we can say that Test-taker Low is demonstrating an ability to master an amount of artificial construction equivalent to 5 (50% x 10), and thus we can assign Test-taker Low an absolute intelligence score of 5. Similarly, Test-taker Middle, by answering 60% of the test questions correctly, is demonstrating an ability to master a level of artificial construction equivalent to 6 (60% x 10) and can be assigned 6 as an absolute intelligence score. And finally, Test-taker High, by answering 70% of the test questions correctly, is demonstrating an ability to master an amount of artificial construction equivalent to 7 (70% x 10) and can be assigned 7 as an absolute intelligence score. The following table summarizes these results:

Time Period	Artificial Construction	Test-taker	Raw Score	Normed Result	Absolute Intelligence Score
		Low	50%	- 1.0 Std Dev	5
1	10	Middle	60%	Mean	6
		High	70%	+ 1.0 Std Dev	7

Absolute Intelligence Score = Artificial Construction x Raw Score

It would be possible to make use of these absolute intelligence scores when doing the population analyses of individual intelligence differences and general intelligence abilities, but of course the conclusions would turn out to be essentially the same, since these analyses hinge upon the relative performance of the members of the population—and whether one starts with normed results or with absolute intelligence scores, the relative comparisons will remain essentially the same. Thus, the incorporation of absolute intelligence scores does not seem to add any further information when considering the intelligence characteristics of the Time 1 population, but as it turns out these scores will be vital when comparing intelligence performance against *other* populations. For instance, it is already apparent that the members of the Time 1 population are universally demonstrating a greater level of measurable intelligence than the members of the Time 0 population, for whom all absolute intelligence scores would have to be marked as zero:

Time Period	Artificial Construction	Test-taker	Raw Score	Normed Result	Absolute Intelligence Score
		Low	50%	- 1.0 Std Dev	0
0	0	Middle	60%	Mean	0
		High	70%	+ 1.0 Std Dev	0
		Low	50%	- 1.0 Std Dev	5
1	10	Middle	60%	Mean	6
		High	70%	+ 1.0 Std Dev	7

Absolute Intelligence Score = Artificial Construction x Raw Score

At Time 2, the entire procedure is repeated—the Time 2 battery of tests is administered to the population, the results are normed, researchers perform various population analyses, etc. And many of the conclusions turn out to be exactly the same as those determined for the Time 1 population, especially conclusions related to individual intelligence differences, correlation with life results, and the impact of genetic factors in determining general intelligence ability. Thus, the intelligence researchers could hardly be blamed for thinking that overall intelligence characteristics have not changed much in going from Time 1 to Time 2, so similar are all their studies and conclusions—studies and conclusions based upon *relative* exam performance *within* the Time 2 population.

But in fact Time 2 does possess a significant difference. This difference shows up in two different ways. First, reflecting the increase in artificial environmental construction, the contents of the Time 2 battery of tests are more varied and more complex than the contents of the Time 1 battery of tests, and yet despite this extra challenge, the Time 2 population has still achieved the same level of raw performance on its particular tests. Second, the absolute intelligence scores of the Time 2 population are greater than those of the Time 1 population, doubling across the board. For instance at Time 2, Test-taker Low answers 50% of the test questions correctly, and since the exam reflects a level of artificial environmental construction measured at 20, Test-taker Low's absolute intelligence score is calculated to be 10 (50% x 20), twice that of the corresponding test taker from Time 1. Time 2's Test-taker Middle receives an absolute intelligence score of 12 (60% x 20) and Time 2's Test-taker High receives an absolute intelligence score of 14 (70% x 20), in each case twice that of the corresponding test taker from Time 1. Thus based upon absolute intelligence scores, the Time 2 population is displaying an overall level of measurable intelligence twice that of the Time 1 population:

Time Period	Artificial Construction	Test-taker	Raw Score	Normed Result	Absolute Intelligence Score
0	0	Low	50%	- 1.0 Std Dev	0
		Middle	60%	Mean	0
		High	70%	+ 1.0 Std Dev	0
1	10	Low	50%	- 1.0 Std Dev	5
		Middle	60%	Mean	6
		High	70%	+ 1.0 Std Dev	7
2	20	Low	50%	- 1.0 Std Dev	10
		Middle	60%	Mean	12
		High	70%	+ 1.0 Std Dev	14

Absolute Intelligence Score = Artificial Construction x Raw Score

This procedure is repeated once more at Time 3. The Time 3 battery of tests is administered, normed and analyzed, and here too, the researchers find that many intelligence characteristics of the Time 3 population are the same as those seen in the previous populations, especially those characteristics connected to the correlations underlying individual intelligence differences and general intelligence ability. This gives the impression that intelligence is, in some sense, stable over time.

But the researchers also note that there are differences at Time 3, differences that are now stark. First, the Time 3 tests, reflecting a five-fold increase in artificial environmental construction from Time 2, are now much more varied and more complex. And yet despite this additional variety and complexity, the Time 3 population still manages to achieve the same level of raw performance on its particular exams. This leads to the other stark difference, a massive leap in absolute intelligence scores. With the battery of tests now reflecting a level of artificial construction measuring 100, Test-taker Low at Time 3, answering 50% of the test questions correctly, achieves an absolute intelligence score of 50 (50% x 100). In similar fashion, Test-taker Middle at Time 3 achieves an absolute intelligence score of 60 (60% x 100), and Test-taker High at Time 3 achieves an absolute intelligence score of 70 (70% x 100). These absolute intelligence scores from Time 3 are considerably greater than all those achieved by the previous populations, suggesting that in an observable sense, intelligence is not stable at all but is instead significantly increasing over time:

Time Period	Artificial Construction	Test-taker	Raw Score	Normed Result	Absolute Intelligence Score
0	0	Low	50%	- 1.0 Std Dev	0
		Middle	60%	Mean	0
		High	70%	+ 1.0 Std Dev	0
1	10	Low	50%	- 1.0 Std Dev	5
		Middle	60%	Mean	6
		High	70%	+ 1.0 Std Dev	7
2	20	Low	50%	- 1.0 Std Dev	10
		Middle	60%	Mean	12
		High	70%	+ 1.0 Std Dev	14
3	100	Low	50%	- 1.0 Std Dev	50
		Middle	60%	Mean	60
		High	70%	+ 1.0 Std Dev	70

Absolute Intelligence Score = Artificial Construction x Raw Score

The question that wants to be asked is this: is human intelligence stable over time or is it instead increasing? But when we examine the circumstances of the scenario, we recognize that the question itself is ambiguous, and betrays a misunderstanding of what human intelligence is. Intelligence is commonly thought of as just a neural ability, but in fact neural ability is only half of the story. In order to understand and to explain the pattern of IQ performance over human history, both as outlined in the scenario and as seen on actual intelligence tests over the past one hundred years, we must expand our definition of intelligence. Measurable human intelligence actually consists of the interaction of two orthogonal factors: one, individual intelligence capacity (that is, neural ability), and two, the total amount of artificial construction contained within the human environment, the target towards which individual intelligence capacity can be applied. Over the course of human history, one of these factors has remained almost entirely stable, while the other factor has been significantly—indeed dramatically—increasing.

Therefore, when we ask whether human intelligence is stable or increasing, we need to clarify first exactly what it is that we are asking. If we are asking is *general intelligence ability* stable or increasing, then the answer to that question is that general intelligence ability is stable over time. This is exactly as we might expect for an ability that is being driven primarily by biological, genetic and neural factors. There is little reason to think that *Homo sapiens* would have undergone a major change in this biological capacity since the earliest days of the species. Thus, the first of the *Homo sapiens* would have had roughly the same intellectual ability as did the later out-of-Africa hunter-gatherers, who in turn would have had roughly the same intellectual ability as did the Mesopotamians, who in turn would have had roughly the same intellectual ability as do modern day humans. This stability shows up in intelligence research, which gives no indication that general intelligence ability has been undergoing any kind of transition over the last one hundred years.

But if we are instead asking is the *measured level of overall intelligence* stable or increasing, then the answer to that question is that the measured level of overall intelligence is increasing over time. This is because the measured level of overall intelligence is determined by more than just general intelligence ability. To *demonstrate* intelligence, general intelligence ability must be *applied* to something, and that something is the artificial construction contained within the environment, or its proxy, the contents of an IQ exam. Furthermore, the greater the amount of environmental artificial construction, the greater the amount of intelligence that can be demonstrated. This was seen throughout the last century, a century in which televisions, computers, airplanes and so much more were being introduced into the human environment, an additional amount of artificial complexity that both was being navigated and mastered by humans in their everyday lives, and also was driving up raw performance on intelligence exams. Ultimately, it is the accruing amount of artificial construction contained within the human environment that determines the overall level of human intelligence, and thus it is this accruing amount of artificial construction that drives the Flynn effect.

It has become quite common in recent years to suggest that the Flynn effect has now plateaued or even reversed. The various studies on this matter have been somewhat conflicting, with some data suggesting that raw intelligence scores are no longer increasing and other data suggesting just the opposite. And of course it should be noted that over a short period of time there is bound to be some statistical noise. But one thing should be certain to us by now. Based upon the above analysis and discussion, and based upon an understanding of human history, there is no reason to expect that the Flynn effect has ended or is reversing. Barring a catastrophe (such as civilization collapse), the human environment will continue to accrue greater and greater amounts of artificial construction, and the future generations will be obliged to navigate and to master this increase in artificial construction, and will thereby go on to demonstrate an increased level of measurable intelligence.

One possible explanation for why the Flynn effect has become more difficult to detect in recent years is that contemporary IQ tests might be failing to keep up with the types of changes that are currently taking place within the human environment. In order for the contents of an IQ test to serve as an accurate proxy for the kind of artificial complexity humans encounter in their everyday lives, those contents must be modified over time to reflect the transitioning environmental circumstances. The popularity of tests such as Stanford-Binet and Wechsler could be biasing researchers on what should serve as the standard type of content for an IQ test, leaving those researchers somewhat blinded to any alternatives. For instance, we already have an example in the Raven's Progressive Matrices, an alternative kind of test focused on geometric and logical pattern, a type of artificiality that increased greatly in the technically and visually enriched world of the twentieth century, and indeed Raven's Progressive Matrices has proven to be not only a good measure of general intelligence ability, it has also experienced some of the greatest Flynn effect movement throughout the last century. And even the so-called standard content of IQ tests betrays that there is really no such thing as a standard when it comes to the type of content that belongs on an intelligence exam. Arithmetic, for instance, might be considered a standard subject now, but there was a time not that long ago when arithmetic did not even exist in the human world. By necessity, the contents of IQ exams must be fluid over time, because an exam's most important requirement is that it reflect the amount and type of artificial complexity that is contained within the human environment, something that is always changing over time.

I can think of two recent changes in human complexity and artificiality that might not be getting adequate representation on current IQ exams. First, there is the notion of multitasking. When I was young, concentrating on one task at a time was considered generally the norm—indeed it was often encouraged—but today, a great deal of human work and play is accomplished by doing a multitude of tasks in parallel. Think of all the office workers who can maintain several open windows on their computer screen, moving seamlessly from chats to emails to spreadsheets, etc. Or think of the teenagers who can engage with multiple applications on their smartphones while maintaining an ongoing conversation with friends. The younger generations, having grown up in a world more suffused with these multitasking demands, generally find such efforts to be easier to accomplish than do the older generations, for whom multitasking still has something of an unfamiliar feel. Nonetheless, multitasking has become an essential skill for navigating the parallel complexity of the modern world, and if this skill were more directly measured on IQ tests, the results would likely reveal not only that multitasking has become an important aspect of modern human intelligence, but also that there is a significant difference in performance between the younger and older generations.

A second area of change in recent environmental complexity is that humans do not interact *directly* with the artificial features of their surrounding world as frequently as they once did, but instead they provide instructions to some type of machine which can handle the interaction for them (often with greater efficiency and accuracy). For instance, humans these days seldom perform arithmetic by hand, as they once commonly did; instead, they program a calculator or computer to accomplish the task for them. This increases the amount of artificial complexity that can be navigated, because a correctly programmed machine can produce a massive leveraging effect. But this also means that humans, to be effective in the current world, must acquire a new set of skills, skills falling under the heading of coding or programming. And once again, it is the younger generations, having been born into a world that more frequently requires these types of machine instruction (just take a look at the current lineup of children's toys) that find such coding tasks to be easier to accomplish than do the older generations, who are in many ways still scrambling to catch up. If machine coding skills were given more attention on the current IQ tests, then the results would likely indicate, much like with multitasking skills, that machine coding is now a critical aspect of human intelligence, and that there is a significant difference in performance between the younger and older generations.

Whether it is through recognition that human intelligence has been increasing in areas not yet commonly measured, or whether it simply takes the passage of enough time, researchers will eventually realize that the Flynn effect is still very much with us here in the early twenty-first century, just as it has always been, and the Flynn effect will continue to shadow humanity throughout the coming years. The Flynn effect is not just a twentieth-century aberration. The increase in human intelligence is instead one of the most fundamental components of the human transformation itself, encompassing the two essential features of that transformation, the artificial reconstruction of the human environment, and the human behavioral responsiveness to that artificial reconstruction. Thus, in a very real and observable sense, human intelligence is *built*—it exists less inside our heads than it does in the surrounding environment. The artificial construction we now observe so abundantly all around us, this is the physical manifestation of intelligence itself, and since the amount and complexity of that artificial construction continues to increase over time, so does human intelligence.

4. The Nature of Autism

Our description and expanded definition of intelligence marks it as the most fundamental human quality underlying the human transformation. The intimate linkage of intelligence to artificial environmental reconstruction, and to the human behavioral responsiveness to that reconstruction, means that the human transformation is in essence the equivalent of the growth in human intelligence. Other human qualities, such as language skills or collective learning, are important because of their leveraging effect, but they are not fundamental. These other qualities are themselves built up out of the constructed artifacts contained within or introduced into the environment, and are thus less basic to the transformative process than intelligence itself. Intelligence essentially *describes* the process, and thus human intelligence, correctly defined, lies at the core of the human transformation.

Nonetheless, intelligence does not explain *why* there has been a human transformation—intelligence is simply part of the description and does not serve as its own cause. And nothing that has been said so far gives an indication of what has prompted humanity to head down this transformative intelligence path, and given that Earth's long biological history has not been witness to any similar transformation before humanity came along, it would seem there must be something unique that has spurred this species to head off in this unusual direction. Intelligence therefore is the *consequence* of something, it is a resultant effect, and thus to discover what has catalyzed, and continues to catalyze, human intelligence and the human transformation, we are going to need to search in an entirely different direction.

To summarize what has been discussed so far, recall first that humans were once pure animals, with the same restrictive survival-and-procreative focus that is experienced by every organism that falls under evolution's domain. As with the other animals, human perception was once tightly constrained, targeted almost entirely towards objects such as food, water, rivals, sexual targets and conspecifics, and thus human perception would have been almost entirely blinded to objects and concepts not serving immediate survival-and-procreative demand. But sometime within the last few hundred thousand years, and accelerating beginning around fifty to one hundred thousand years ago, humans began to break free of evolution's constraints, by turning evolution's process inside out and by reconstructing the human surroundings entirely for human benefit. These reconstructions can be characterized almost entirely by the word *artificial*, they rely heavily upon the structural concepts of pattern, symmetry, repetition, logic, number and form. If you look deeply into any human artifact—a building, a word, a computer chip—what you will discover is an innovative use of pattern, structure and form not typically seen in the biological world. Humans can now make these innovations because humans now *perceive* the structure that underlies them; humans have become adept at visualizing their world in a way that goes beyond just the biological and the evolutionary, that goes beyond just a restrictive focus on food, water, rivals, etc. So the question to be asked is, what has sparked this broadened perceptual awareness? Is there some feature, some characteristic, unique to the human population and observable within that population, that has prompted humanity to enlarge its perceptual boundaries, to break free of evolution's perceptual constraints, to see much further than just survival-and-procreative demand?

The answer to that question is yes. There is indeed an observable and significantly present feature within the human population that has had the impact, and continues to have the impact, of broadening human perception. Furthermore, this feature's perceptual characteristics are exactly those one would expect in accounting for the characteristics of the human transformation, namely a heightened awareness of underlying pattern, structure and form, accompanied by a diminished awareness of the survival-and-procreative world. This feature can be denoted with just one word, but I hesitate to mention that word. I suspect if every word in the English language were to be ranked in the order of its likelihood for being the underlying impetus behind the human transformation, nearly everyone would put this word somewhere near the bottom of their list. It is a word that is poorly understood. It is a word that has been mostly mischaracterized. So our first order of business will be to examine this word more carefully, to dig more deeply into its true nature, and to discover why this word is the key for explaining the perceptual changes that have been catalyzing the human transformation.

That one word is *autism*.

Autism as a word did not come into existence until the twentieth century. It was first used in the early 1900s by the German psychiatrist Eugene Bleuler in describing the more withdrawn characteristics of schizophrenic patients. Then nearly simultaneously in the 1940s, American psychiatrist Leo Kanner and Austrian pediatrician Hans Asperger employed the adjective *autistic* in their published case studies of children who were displaying a distinct set of behavioral features—namely language peculiarities, social difficulties, and obsessive engagement with unusual activities and interests. This set of behavioral features became the basis for the definition of what was thereafter recognized to be a distinct and lifelong condition, the condition now known as autism.

Although the case studies of Kanner and Asperger did include instances where the prognosis and outcome were not all that dire, during the 1950s and 1960s autism was recognized, studied and regarded almost invariably as a devastating medical condition. Outcomes were assumed to be poor, with institutionalization often regarded as inevitable, and treatments could be draconian. Autism at that time was assumed to be an extremely rare occurrence, with prevalence estimates running as low as one in ten thousand (0.01%).

These estimates would change greatly throughout the final three decades of the twentieth century, with autism becoming more and more frequently recognized and diagnosed. By the year 2000, prevalence studies were estimating that the incidence of autism was somewhere around 1 in 150 (0.67%). The main driver in this increased recognition of autism was a growing awareness that not every instance had to be severe and not every outcome had to be poor. Children were being diagnosed as having all the telltale characteristics of autism but with those characteristics ranging widely in both detail and intensity, and often easing, sometimes dramatically, with time. Terms such as *high-functioning autism* and *Asperger's Syndrome* were invented to delineate the more promising cases from those considered to be more "classic," although the distinction between these terms was never clearly defined. Indeed, it was a confusing era for autism, with large disagreement over the meaning of the condition. The increased prevalence, combined with a lingering attitude that autism was something to be regarded as both medical and tragic, induced general fear that autism had become an epidemic within the population. Funding and research were exponentially increased, targeted almost always towards discovering both a cause and a cure. At the same time, countering voices were growing louder—including voices from autistic individuals—saying that autism was being unfairly demonized and grossly misunderstood.

Since the year 2000, attitudes and prevalence have continued to undergo major revision. Some consensus has formed around the notion that autism should be described as a spectrum, meaning that although every autistic individual exhibits to an observable degree the defining features of the condition, there is an extremely broad range of variation in both presentation and outcome. Some autistic individuals will experience more intensely the characteristics associated with autism, and will struggle to achieve independent lives, although this outcome still appears to be relatively rare. Many autistic individuals will manage to achieve some level of acclimation to their condition and will become participating members within the population, sometimes with additional support and sometimes with complete independence. There are now many examples of autistic individuals having succeeded in college, having gone on to marry and to raise families, having gained successful careers, and so on. Recently there has even been a movement in some industries, such as computer software development, to actively seek out autistic individuals for the work value of their particular characteristics. Recent prevalence studies have indicated that nearly 1 in 50 children (2.0%) are being identified as autistic by the age of eight. This high level of prevalence, combined with a growing recognition that many autistic individuals lead successful and productive lives, has helped bolster an understanding that autism likely did not spring up out of nowhere during the twentieth century, but instead that autistic individuals have been a significant presence within the human population for quite some time. Individuals once commonly described as quirky, eccentric, isolated, etc., they are now being more frequently recognized as autistic.

Despite these ongoing changes in both prevalence estimates and how autism is being generally regarded, the medical and academic communities still seem to be struggling to catch up. Research and funding have continued to be focused almost exclusively on autism as a medical condition, with treatment and cure still frequently promulgated as the ultimate goal. These attempts to uncover the medical root cause of autism have branched off into several different avenues of pursuit. One line of research has focused on autism as being a hereditary disorder, a hypothesis suggested by the fact that identical twin and other family studies have indicated a genetic underpinning for the condition. A second line of research has targeted autism as a neurological aberration, a thesis being tested through an assortment of neuroimaging studies, mostly centered around detecting atypical brain signatures in autistic individuals. Finally, autism as a metabolic condition has also received a great deal of attention and effort, as have theories suggesting a variety of environmental insults, with everything from vaccines to highway pollution being put forth as the primary trigger of disease.

The persistence of these efforts is reflected in the growing autism research literature, which has expanded by at least an order of magnitude in the last two decades alone. A recent listing of such efforts would include the following titles: *Autism spectrum disorder symptom expression in individuals with 3q29 deletion syndrome*; *Cortical thickness abnormalities in autism spectrum disorder*; and *Metabolomic Signatures of Autism Spectrum Disorder*. These and other representative articles demonstrate the degree to which the current research continues to focus on genetics, neurons and metabolic pathways, as well as on the pursuit of treatment and cure. But there is a growing irony haunting these many efforts, an irony that can be recognized by considering a sampling of research articles from the early 2000s: *Examination of AVPR1a as an autism susceptibility gene;*

Neuroanatomic variation in monozygotic twin pairs discordant for the narrow phenotype for autism; and *Mercury exposure in children with autistic spectrum disorder.* That is to say, not much has changed in autism research over the last several decades, other than a great expansion in volume and a constant shifting of the targeted culprits. Each year new candidate genes, new neural pathways, new metabolic mechanisms and new environmental triggers are put forth with great fanfare and considerable promise, which are then followed by years in which their mention gradually declines. New therapies and new drugs are frequently introduced and promoted, but then fail to deliver any significant results in any unbiased trial. Watching this futile cycle play out again and again, year after year, decade after decade, one eventually gets the sense that when it comes to autism, the medical and academic communities are essentially spinning their wheels. And if there is to be any conclusion drawn from the autism research to date, it is that we have every reason to suspect that autism is *not* a medical condition.

In my opinion, one of the more effective ways to achieve a greater understanding of autism is to begin by exploring what it means to be non-autistic, which is to say, what it means to be biologically typical. This is not exactly an unfamiliar topic to this discussion, because in a certain sense humans were most biologically typical when they were in the state of being pure animals, with both their behaviors and their perceptions shaped almost exclusively by survival-and-procreative demand; the biological norm is to have all of one's effort and attention directed towards the immediate essentials—food, water, rivals, sex, etc. Of course this biologically pure state no longer entirely pertains for modern humans, including non-autistic modern humans, but it is nonetheless important to recognize how the carryover from this animal past continues to influence behavior and perception in modern times. For most humans today, despite finding themselves nearly fully immersed in an artificially constructed environment, and despite having nearly all their biological needs easily and abundantly met, they nonetheless still find themselves giving a great deal of attention and effort to the familiar targets—food, water, rivals, sex, etc. Many of us can confirm this proclivity simply by examining our own thoughts and actions, and in addition, a general look at some of the more popular human activities and interests will further reveal the extent to which humans have remained strongly preoccupied with their more primitive and natural selves. Everything from soap operas to scatological humor to crosstown sports rivalries betrays the degree to which humans have continued to be fascinated with the animal aspect of humankind. There is nothing surprising or maladjusted about any of these tendencies, they are in fact entirely to be expected. They are the natural consequence of humans being not all that far removed from a former purely animal state.

One of the more intriguing components of humanity's carryover from its animal past is the notion of conspecific perception. Conspecific perception is the natural tendency for organisms to possess a heightened perceptual awareness for the other members of their own species. For instance, lions perceive first and foremost other lions, honeybees perceive first and foremost other honeybees, etc. And of course humans perceive first and foremost other humans. When one walks into a conference room, despite one's visual field being almost entirely filled with various non-human artifacts, one's attention is nonetheless drawn immediately and naturally to the other humans already in the room. This intensified intra-species recognition is evolutionarily fundamental and essential for a number of reasons. First, successful mating requires a physical connection with another member of the same species, an occurrence that would be haphazard at best without an enhanced perception for one's own kind. Also, the rearing of young would be utterly ineffective if either parent or offspring could not easily identify and perceptually foreground the other—imagine the consequences of a mother unable to distinguish her own brood from the broods of other species, or a litter unable to discern and to imitate its elders. In addition, many species coalesce into physical and geographical groups for warmth, for effective pack hunting, for more tenacious defense and so on, with these groupings themselves the evidence of how each member is more greatly attuned to the presence and activities of the others in the species. Conspecific perception is crucial to successful survival and procreation, so much so that it should probably be included within the definition of what it means to be a species.

In humans, conspecific perception is quite strong, as would be the case for almost any species considered to be social, and the strength of this human form of conspecific perception is most apparent when considering the developmental activities of the very young. Human newborns come into this world quite early and quite helpless, and their first year or two of development is essentially an ongoing scramble to gain a functional foothold. Careful observation of these early years reveals the extent to which human newborns both rely upon and are deeply attuned to the presence and activities of other humans: a mother's soothing voice, a father's reassuring touch, the smiling gestures of familiar faces. Nearly every child responds immediately, favorably and naturally to these intra-species impressions. And note how critical this process must be in giving the newborn his or her sensory grounding, because without a strong dose of conspecific perception the surrounding environment would most likely emerge as nothing but a cacophony of random sensations: a wild mix of colors and shapes in the visual field, a buzzing range of tones and intensities inside the ear, a chaos of temperatures and impressions upon the skin, and a kaleidoscope of haphazard tastes and smells. Which of these impressions are to be latched upon as important, and which of them can be ignored? Which sensations should be promoted to the perceptual foreground, and which can be discarded into the undiscerned remainder? It is primarily conspecific perception that provides the organizational grounding around which a newborn's sensory world can be arranged. From out of the chaos of countless sensations there emerges a human-forward world: human faces, human laughter, human touch, human smells, human activities. Everything associable to the human species gets a natural preference in the newborn's sensory field, thereby guaranteeing that the newborn's burgeoning perceptual world will become first and foremost a *human* world.

In addition to conspecific perception's primary impact of providing sensory and developmental grounding, an impact shared in common with almost every other animal species, conspecific perception in humans now also serves a secondary purpose, that of providing a species-wide awareness of the new features and behaviors being brought forth by the human transformation. When one thinks of the many structured artifacts and exploits that now dominate the human landscape—a rattle, a book, a university lecture—one might wonder at first why humans would give any attention at all to these artificial impressions, given that there is no natural incentive to do so. These objects and activities are not food, they are not water, they are not sex, etc., and thus in the natural world, in the world of pure animals, these objects and activities would seem destined to become part of the undistinguished perceptual background. But of course the reason these strange artifacts and behaviors end up garnering a great deal of human attention, including the attention of humans of a very young age, is that these artifacts and behaviors have become intimately connected to the human species itself. Humans touch these artifacts, humans point at these artifacts, humans put these artifacts into other people's hands. Thus, once an artificial object or behavior has gained sufficient foothold to become part of the fabric of human experience, that object or behavior gets promoted to the human perceptual foreground, because conspecific perception gives humans the natural inclination to pay attention to what other humans do.

Therefore, a large part of what it means to be biologically typical is to participate in an immense and shared perceptual network of human-centric features and behaviors, some of which date back to the species' purely animal past, and some of which correspond to the changes of modern times. Humans eat what other humans eat, humans fear what other humans fear, and humans gather where other humans are. And furthermore, when one human makes a gesture, or utters a word, or scribbles something down, there will be other humans standing nearby and paying the closest of attention, supporting the entire range of constructed artifacts and behaviors that fall under the heading of human language. And when one human points to the heavenly bodies, or narrates the tribe's origin story, or demonstrates the workings of the newest innovation, there will be other humans avidly watching and listening, reinforcing a broad array of structured behaviors that constitute collective learning. The continuity of human behavior, as well as the continuity of the human environment—including those activities and features arising out of the human transformation—all ride on a sea of conspecific perception, the natural glue holding together the species and its actions.

Since conspecific perception is so clearly crucial to both human development and to the species-wide awareness supporting the many features defining the human transformation, it raises an interesting question about what would happen if a member of the species did not possess a strong sense of conspecific perception. What would be the developmental consequence of a newborn coming into this world less able than other humans to perceptually foreground the human aspects of the surrounding environment, and what would be the overall ramifications of an individual not able to obtain his or her sensory grounding from a human-forward world? This is not really a theoretical question, because I believe we already know the answer. Any member of the human species possessing a weakened sense of conspecific perception, any human less able than other humans to perceptually foreground the human aspects of the surrounding environment, any individual unable to obtain his or her sensory grounding from a human-forward world, that individual would be most accurately described as autistic.

One of the chief defining characteristics of autism is that autistic individuals experience a broad assortment of what are usually described as social difficulties: lack of eye contact, unwillingness to participate in reciprocal play or sharing, failure to point or to follow the pointing of others, reluctance to engage in small talk and in other forms of social interaction, etc. The autism research literature has tended to blame these difficulties on presumed deficits in some proposed biological or neurological mechanism, but I would suggest that these long-standing conjectures are incorrect on two different fronts—one, these conjectures are mischaracterizing the conduct, and two, they are understating its cause. When one observes carefully the actual activities of autistic individuals, and especially the activities of very young autistic individuals, it becomes quickly apparent that these individuals are to a significant degree *disengaged* from the other humans around them. Whereas most children will readily interact with other people—laugh with them, play with them, follow enthusiastically their every gesture, touch and sound—autistic individuals by contrast seem largely unattuned to the presence of other humans. Autistic toddlers often do not respond to their name being called, and can be seen as being reluctant and awkward with such things as hugs and coos. Young autistic children attend less to other people than to favorite objects and interests. Autistic adolescents seldom pursue the range of friendships and relationships that other adolescents usually do. And even autistic adults, many of whom have become reasonably acclimated by then to various social customs and expectations, will nonetheless often describe their inner experience as one of extreme isolation and alienation. Thus, autistic individuals are not demonstrating specific social deficits so much as they are demonstrating a broad-scale disinclination towards the members of their own species, and it is this broad-scale disinclination that accounts for the various social difficulties. But a broad-scale disinclination towards the members of one's own species is the same thing as saying that an autistic individual is experiencing a weakened sense of conspecific perception. Unlike biologically typical humans, who will quite naturally perceive first and foremost other people, autistic individuals do not possess this natural tendency, and thus theirs is not first and foremost a *human* world.

That autistic individuals are dealing with a weakened sense of conspecific perception is evidenced also by the frequency with which these individuals experience an assortment of sensory issues. Many autistic individuals report a wide and non-specific range of sensory symptoms: for instance, being overwhelmed by the intensity of various textures, noises and smells (hypersensitivity); or being oblivious to extreme sensations, such as a shouted name or the sudden onset of hot and cold (hyposensitivity); or a commingling of the senses, such as "seeing" tones or "feeling" colors (synesthesia). The motleyness of these sensory symptoms suggests that they are not the result of any specific physical defect but are instead the consequence of a more general difficulty in obtaining sensory grounding. Biologically typical children rely upon conspecific perception to organize their otherwise chaotic array of sensory impressions, favoring and foregrounding those experiences that are in some way connected to the human species. But autistic individuals, not very aware of other people and not naturally favoring human-associated impressions, find themselves dealing with what must seem to be an overwhelming cascade of random and chaotic sensations, with no clearcut means for achieving sensory organization or cementing a sensory grounding, resulting in the many observed sensory issues as well as in a delay of perceptual development.

This weakness in conspecific perception can vary greatly from individual to individual, and this is perhaps one of the reasons that autism presents as a spectrum. Some autistic individuals appear to be almost entirely lacking in perceptual attachment to human presence, and these individuals can be seen as facing the greater challenge in achieving developmental gains. Other autistic individuals do seem to retain some level of connection and perceptual awareness for other humans—albeit much less than that of their biologically typical peers—and these individuals would appear to have the better chance of reaching independence and well-being. But despite the variation, there is nonetheless a threshold that would appear to be critical in determining the autistic/non-autistic divide. Any human individual with a strong enough sense of conspecific perception to be able to make use of that perception to achieve his or her sensory grounding, that individual is to be classified as non-autistic. Such an individual will strongly attach to the human species itself and will begin to see the surrounding world in much the same way as other humans do. And in the modern world, such an individual will be able to leverage this human connection into the realms of language and collective learning, where conspecific perception plays such an important role, and the individual will by these means begin to easily follow the same developmental path being traveled by the large majority of the population.

In contrast, any individual with a sense of conspecific perception so weak as to be unable to use that perception to achieve a strong sensory grounding, that individual is to be classified as autistic. Such individuals will find themselves dealing at first with something akin to a sensory chaos, since there will be few prominent features, such as other humans, naturally standing out from the manifold of sensory impressions. Such individuals will thus be cut off from the typical form of sensory organization and will not be able to easily follow the same developmental path as their biologically typical peers. Such individuals will not be able to perceive their surrounding environment in the same way as other humans do.

And this at last gets us to the heart of the matter, the key to why autism is so critical for understanding the spark underlying the human transformation. Biologically typical humans experience a world that is organized primarily around the human species and its members, biologically typical humans perceive first and foremost a species-centric world. Autistic individuals do not primarily perceive this species-centric world, and thus what they tend to perceive is something entirely different. And that is the critical question: what exactly is it that autistic individuals tend to perceive?

Another chief defining characteristic of autism is that autistic individuals frequently engage in what are usually described as restricted and repetitive behaviors and interests. In young autistic children, examples of these behaviors and interests cover a broad range of curious activities: hand flapping, lining up toys, eating the same food for every meal, obsession with certain objects such as ceiling fans and light switches, resistance to furniture rearrangement or to changes in a geographical route, strict adherence to ritual and to order in activities such as dressing, and so on. Later on in life, autistic adolescents will commonly focus much of their time and energy on a limited set of particular interests, such as sports statistics or dinosaurs or the weather, and will often perseverate (talk constantly) about a favorite topic. Autistic adults can sometimes be seen as leveraging their interests into studies and careers, with the stereotypical target of these efforts being those activities known for their rigid structure and rules: mathematics, physics, chess, computer programming, etc. A large amount of autism treatment is aimed at suppressing these various behaviors and interests, because much of the autism research community still regards these activities as anti-productive and harmful. But in a manner ranging all the way from screaming tantrums to the most eloquent of postings placed online, autistic individuals can be observed forcefully resisting these many attempts at suppression. And indeed, when one watches carefully the so-called restricted and repetitive behaviors and interests of autistic individuals, it is hard not to come away with the impression that for such individuals these behaviors and interests are utterly necessary, as though serving an essential purpose.

That essential purpose is the obtaining of a sensory grounding. When one considers the circumstance of an autistic individual not possessing a strong sense of conspecific perception, and in particular not able to make use of conspecific perception to help with sensory organization, one recognizes that this individual is facing the most precarious of outcomes. As has been described previously, unfiltered sensory impressions are apt to be experienced as both chaotic and overwhelming: the wild mix of colors and shapes in the visual field, the buzzing range of tones and intensities inside the ear, the chaos of temperatures and impressions upon the skin, and the kaleidoscope of haphazard tastes and smells. If these sensory circumstances were to remain unresolved, the autistic individual would be unable to obtain any perceptual signal from the sensory environment and would be left with only sensory noise. In turn this would mean that the barriers to developmental progress would be set impossibly high. But most autistic individuals do not end up experiencing this extreme outcome. We know that most autistic individuals do manage to make significant developmental progress, even if somewhat delayed compared to their non-autistic peers, and many autistic individuals do go on to become participating and productive members within the general population, navigating quite successfully the features of a modern human world. So these individuals have not become stuck inside a sensory chaos and must therefore be achieving a functional degree of sensory organization. But if that sensory organization has not been built around conspecific perception, then what has it been built around?

The trick here is to recognize that I have not been exactly forthcoming by characterizing the sensory field as entirely random. On the planet Earth, the sensory field, although indeed wildly multivariate, still possesses within itself a great deal of inherent structure and form. In addition to the biological structure imparted by the evolutionary propensity towards food, water, conspecifics and the like—the structural organization that most organisms latch onto quite naturally—there is also a great deal of structure that arises from such influences as gravity, chemistry, thermodynamics, celestial cycles, etc. Trees grow tall in a straight line, mountain peaks have a particular shape, water drips in a rhythm, the moon cycles through regular phases, and of course in the modern world artificial structure can be found practically everywhere. These non-biological instances of environmental structure and form are captured in a variety of words and concepts: symmetry, pattern, repetition, logic, number. These concepts possess one characteristic in common, they are all chaos-defying features. In the sensory world, these are the elements that serve to break the background noise.

The interesting thing is, for most biological organisms, they never seem to become aware of these non-biological structural features, never become aware of the many instances of symmetry, pattern, repetition and so on. It can be surmised that the reason for this lack of awareness of non-biological structure is that it is not strictly necessary for survival and procreation. Having successfully organized their sensory experience into a biologically and conspecifically guided form of perception, and having had their fitness greatly boosted by this particular form of perception, most organisms then find themselves locked into that way of perceiving their world, remaining almost entirely blind to any other type of structure their world might happen to contain.

But for autistic individuals, less able to organize their sensory experience around the usual biological concepts—including most particularly around the notion of conspecific perception—and at risk for the dire developmental consequence that would result from a persistent sensory chaos, they will latch onto any alternative means of sensory organization that happens to be available. Therefore, autistic individuals, unlike their biologically typical peers, will find themselves becoming directly aware of non-biological structure and form, will find themselves becoming directly aware of symmetry, pattern, repetition, logic, number and so on. From the pressing need to resolve their potential sensory chaos, autistic individuals will begin to hone in on those environmental features that serve to break the background noise.

That autistic individuals are embracing this alternative perceptual path is most evident from their so-called restricted and repetitive behaviors and interests. These activities are not arbitrary, but indeed have a requisite quality to them—all promote and enhance the non-biological structure that an autistic individual has begun to crave. Hand flapping is rhythmic to both sight and touch, every routine is a repetition. Ceiling fans encompass both symmetrical shape and regular motion, light switches capture a logic. And note the distinction in the use of toys, for instance in a set of dolls and dishes. The biologically typical child might easily be found sharing such toys with other children, setting out perhaps the scenario of an afternoon tea party, the type of interactive play that rides so firmly upon the shoulders of conspecific perception. But the autistic child is much more likely to line up these toys, or form them into a circle or some other patterned shape, carving out yet one more instance of non-biological structure in the child's sensory field. The restricted and repetitive behaviors and interests of autistic individuals serve an essential purpose, they bring forward the non-biological structure inherently contained in the surrounding environment, they enhance the perceptual experience of symmetry, pattern, repetition, logic, number and so on. They bring organization to the autistic individual's sensory world.

These days, biologically typical children chart a developmental path that begins, via the mechanism of conspecific perception, with a strong association to humankind. And because the many humans they encounter and observe along the way are also engaged with the artifacts and behaviors of a complex structural world—a world that has gone far beyond just the immediate needs of survival and procreation—these biologically typical children, naturally curious about what other humans do, soon begin to participate in this complex structural world too. Suppression of this developmental path would be predictably disastrous. If a biologically typical child were to be cut off entirely from human contact and were to be given no opportunity to leverage conspecific perception, then not only would this child be deprived of his or her preferred and natural way of perceiving the environment, this child would also be deprived of his or her most straightforward connection to the expanded structural aspects of the modern world. Fortunately, very few biologically typical children encounter such cruelty, with most today making excellent developmental progress, eventually transitioning to becoming fully contributing members of a complex human society.

By way of comparison, autistic children employ the same developmental path as do biologically typical children, but autistic children traverse this path in the opposite direction. Autistic children gain their sensory grounding first through an awareness and manipulation of the non-biological and structural aspects of their surrounding world. And because much of this structural world has been integrated to humankind, and because this structural world depends in many ways upon human interaction, autistic individuals—perhaps reluctantly at first—eventually progress to that awkward but helpful moment when they begin to attach themselves to the members of their own species. Here too, suppression of this developmental path would be predictably disastrous. If an autistic child were to be cut off from his or her structured behaviors and interests, then not only would this child be deprived of his or her preferred and natural way of perceiving the environment, this child would also be deprived of his or her most straightforward connection to a human-centric world. Unfortunately, far too many autistic children are actually subjected to this kind of cruelty. Many of the so-called treatments and therapies for autism are designed specifically to force the autistic child to abandon his or her preferred way of perceiving the environment, attempting to substitute instead the perceptual preferences of biologically typical children. And this is such a shame. The developmental path from autistic perception to eventual engagement with a human-centric world can be traversed successfully and yield productive results. It is the reason many autistic individuals end up making excellent developmental progress, eventually transitioning to becoming fully contributing members of a complex human society.

This then is the nature of autism. It begins with a weakened sense of conspecific perception, weak enough that it will stymie the autistic individual from organizing his or her sensory experience around other humans and what other humans do. This circumstance often results in developmental delays, it often results in sensory issues. But in compensation, the autistic individual will find himself or herself latching onto the inherent structure contained within the surrounding environment, latching onto the many examples of symmetry, pattern, repetition, logic, number and form. And where have we heard those words before, what role have they been playing in the discussion? Were these not the words considered critical for understanding the human transformation?

Autism is a variable path—some autistic individuals will struggle mightily to make developmental progress, others will do remarkably well. But all autistic individuals have an important influence on humankind, because all help bring to the species *Homo sapiens* a new and revolutionary form of perception.

5. Shedding Light on the Riddle

A few hundred thousand years ago, the dynamic of biological life on Earth would have had a familiar and predictable quality to it. All organisms were earnestly engaged in the struggle for survival and procreation, as had been the case for many hundreds of millions of years, and other than the usually slow-moving drift afforded by geological change and genetic alteration, each species would have found itself proceeding with a remarkable similarity and an unyielding regularity. Birth and death, eating and drinking, fighting and fleeing, procreating and nurturing—day after day, generation after generation, millennium after millennium. Much like today's TV nature shows, the plot line was always the same. Caught in a vice grip of evolutionary constraint, each member of each species remained locked inside the same general set of rigid behaviors, behaviors absolutely essential for biological continuation, but also utterly tyrannical towards any alternative.

At the heart of these rigid behaviors was to be found a set of sensory and perceptual characteristics just as constrained as the activities they engendered. Each organism was keenly focused on those evolutionarily essential features to be found in the surrounding environment—food, water, predators, rivals, sexual targets—and this intense sensory focus included the notion of conspecific perception, the tendency for each organism to have an enhanced and preferential awareness for the other members of its own species. The upshot of these sensory and perceptual characteristics was a constant reinforcement of a universal consistency. Cognizant of only those environmental features satisfying biological

81

demand, and taking its cues from and copying the behaviors of the other similarly constrained members of the species population, each organism was experiencing its world in nearly the exact same way. Each organism was perceiving its surrounding environment through the same biologically filtered lens, a lens helping to enforce the strict regularity and unrelenting continuity that can be observed across nearly every animal species. And note what was *not* being perceived. The non-biological structure contained in the surrounding environment, those many instances of symmetry, pattern, repetition, etc.—the regulative impact of gravity, the recurrent cycles of celestial bodies, the logical causation of meteorological events—it would appear that these many instances of non-biological structure were seldom reaching any organism's ken, certainly not to the degree to have any significant impact on either organism or species behavior. Thus, whatever useful information the non-biological structural world might have had to impart to biological life on Earth, that information was remaining entirely shrouded within an undiscerned sensory background.

It is important to remember that a few hundred thousand years ago, these statements would have applied just as equally to humans as to every other animal species. For nearly seven million years by then, the hominin lines had been living a purely animal existence, with no indication their behavioral or perceptual experience was fundamentally different from that of the other creatures. Biologically captivated, and corralled into a generational constancy via conspecific perception, humans found themselves tightly ensnared inside a familiar cycle. Birth and death, eating and drinking, fighting and fleeing, procreating and nurturing—day after day, generation after generation, millennium after millennium. And at a few hundred thousand years ago, all that could have been anticipated for humans would have been a continuation along this same path, a continuation for perhaps many more millions of years, with only the subtlest of change being allowed through evolutionary means. Nothing else could have been anticipated because evolutionary constraint had never allowed a significant deviation even once, not for hominins over millions of years, and not for any other species since the beginning of life itself.

That humans did not continue along this same path is biologically extraordinary. That humans freed themselves from evolution's behavioral and perceptual constraints is biologically radical. And that humans, in such a short period of time, managed to reconstruct their environment into the artificial dominion we live within today is nothing short of biologically shocking. Whatever sparked humanity's radical deviation, it could not have been subtle, and it was almost certainly not evolutionary. Whatever sparked humanity's radical deviation could have only been atypical and subversive—atypical and subversive enough to smash evolution's formidable chains.

What I would propose is this. Humans became the first species to sustain a significant percentage of autistic individuals within its population, significant enough to allow the perceptual characteristics of those individuals to begin to influence the perceptual characteristics of the population as a whole.

Without an autistic influence, it can be expected that human perception would have remained tightly and biologically constrained, just as it had been for quite some time, with each individual's sensory focus directed almost exclusively towards the biological features contained within the surrounding environment and towards the other members of the species. Humans still experience the impact of this form of perception to this very day—it is the reason so much of our current attention is still given over to food, danger, sex and the like, and also to other people. What has changed today is that humans now also perceive so much more—symmetry, pattern, repetition, number, logic, etc.—all the structural scaffolding that underlies the artificial construction that has been accumulating all around us. But where could this supplemental form of perception have come from, how did it originate? Biologically typical humans are not prone to perceiving the non-biological structure contained within the surrounding environment, because the restrictive power of biological and conspecific perception is such that it has always relegated alternative forms of structure to the sensory background. Thus, on their own, biologically typical humans do not naturally perceive underlying symmetry, pattern, repetition, number, logic, etc.

But autistic individuals do naturally perceive this underlying non-biological structure. The ironic cunning of the nature of autism, a condition that presents significant survival-and-procreative challenges, is that it also attacks evolutionary constraint right at its very core. Weakened

83

in their degree of conspecific perception and needing somehow to organize their sensory world, autistic individuals end up evading the usual sensory constraints, and instead become naturally drawn to perceiving the non-biological structure in their surrounding environment. Furthermore, autistic individuals do more than just perceive this surrounding structure, they are also driven to recreate it, through their so-called repetitive behaviors and interests. If we could see back to the beginning, we might witness the effects of gravity being mirrored in straight lines drawn upon the ground, or the repetition of dripping water being echoed by rhythmically clapping hands—perhaps the first instances of artificial construction to be introduced into the human environment. It is of course not possible to say for certain just exactly how the first instances of autistic influence manifested within the population, a process that was likely slow and halting at first. But if we are looking for the subversive spark that sent humans cascading down this alternative perceptual path, it cannot be to the biologically typical population that we turn our gaze, a population that had been enjoined from any alternative form of perception for millions of years. Instead, we must turn to the autistic population, where we find exactly the characteristic we are looking for, namely an inherent compulsion towards non-biological perception and towards artificially structured behavior, a compulsion we can witness with our own eyes today.

Although autistic individuals are almost certainly the originators of non-biological perception in humanity, it is also important to recognize that autistic influence is such that it catalyzes non-biological perception in the population as a whole. That is, given a large enough and stable enough presence of autistic individuals, the non-autistic members of the population will also over time begin to perceive underlying non-biological structure and to adopt many of the autism-inspired artificially structured behaviors.

There are two major factors driving this non-autistic adoption of autistic perceptions and behaviors. The first factor is conspecific perception. Biologically typical humans have a keen eye for noticing what other humans do. Of course when every human is biologically typical, then what each observes is the same set of restricted biological and evolutionary behaviors, and nothing generally changes over time. But if there is a significant presence of autistic individuals within the population, those individuals will be providing something entirely new to observe. Thus, when an autistic individual draws a symmetrical figure upon the ground, or claps his hands with staccato, or pantomimes the motions to spark a fire, or points incessantly in the same direction as the wind, there will be other humans standing nearby and paying rapt attention, perhaps preparing themselves to imitate the behavior. Furthermore, if some of these new behaviors suggest the opportunity for better eating or for better shelter or for better sexual and nurturing result, the biologically typical humans, ever alert for survival-and-procreative advantage, will find themselves paying even more attention, with an even greater incentive to copy the behavior. The strength of conspecific perception in biologically typical humans means that autistic behaviors will seldom go unobserved. Neither will go unobserved the products of those autistic behaviors, the many varieties and instances of artificial construction.

The second major factor driving non-autistic adoption of autistic perceptions and behaviors is that the artificial construction created thereby tends to be more or less permanent, meaning that it can serve as an ongoing and accumulating signpost for present and future generations. For instance, a tool or weapon honed into a more symmetrical point or patterned shape becomes itself an enduring fixture in the surrounding environment, with its underlying structure now continuously on display for anyone who uses the artifact or observes its use by others. Therefore, over time, these examples of underlying non-biological structure begin to amass within the human world, with each generation becoming increasingly practiced at both seeing and mastering this structure. Note how different this is from the passing along of biological and evolutionary perceptions and behaviors. Very little about biological behavior is actually etched with any permanency into the surrounding environment; most biological behavior is either instinctive or is learned via the mechanism of conspecific perception, meaning that each generation essentially starts afresh, with no accretive changes over time. In contrast, the enduring nature of artificial construction means that each new generation is born into a world with a larger amount of non-biological structure than was available to previous generations, and this has the persistent impact of nudging the population to greater perception and greater mastery of this structure. We should in fact recognize the concept—this is exactly the process identified previously as the essence of human intelligence, and in the very early days of autistic influence, these first instances of increased recognition and expanding mastery of accumulating artificial construction would have marked the very beginning of the Flynn effect.

The result of these two factors is that over time overall human perception becomes more and more a blend of its two separate sources of influence. Biological perception of course remains strong, as it must for a species that still needs to survive and procreate. But alongside biological perception there now grows a new way of perceiving the world, a way that focuses more on non-biological structure and leans heavily upon accumulating artificial construction, each the consequence of autistic influence. Today, in the modern world, these two forms of perception have become so thoroughly blended that we might easily mistake them for one, and it is only in the extremely young that we still encounter a purer form of each source of influence. It is only around the age of two or three that it is still relatively easy to separate the biologically typical, who are naturally fascinated with other humans and what other humans do, from the autistically atypical, who are less attentive to other humans but more comfortably engaged with the structural aspects of their surrounding world. But as each individual matures and comes under the influence of a human world mixing both autistic and non-autistic characteristics, each individual becomes increasingly dexterous with each type of perception and each type of behavior, making it more and more difficult to tease the influences apart. In today's world, it is extremely rare to find a human adult that can be described as being purely autistic or purely non-autistic; most humans today display perceptual and behavioral characteristics that combine the traits of both, even when it remains obvious which of these traits is the more natural bent.

This might be a good time to remind ourselves that the consequence of this blended form of perception has not been trivial. No longer locked into just a biological/evolutionary way of perceiving its world, humanity has unleashed upon the planet Earth the most stunning of revolutions, a revolution on par with the formation of the chemical elements, the coming together of galactic systems, and the origination of life itself. The products of this revolution are all unprecedented: freedom from evolutionary constraint, an immense landscape of artificial construction, an ongoing growth in human intelligence—all the result of unveiling and making use of the non-biological structure contained within the surrounding environment, an ability sparked at the very moment humanity began to experience the autistic way of perceiving its surrounding world.

As intriguing as it is to consider the earliest days of autistic influence, it is still more illuminating to recognize that this influence has remained ongoing ever since and continues unabated through the present day. Artificial construction continues to accumulate rapidly in the current environment, human intelligence advances measurably with each new generation, and human freedom from evolutionary constraint becomes more and more established with each passing day. The same catalyst that introduced non-biological perception into the species and sparked a remarkable population-wide behavioral revolution is still driving innovation and progress in the modern world. Therefore, the most straightforward way to assess the role autism must be playing in this ongoing revolution is to observe autism's impact on human perceptual and behavioral change today.

In my opinion, one of the more fruitful ways in which to observe recent autistic influence can be found in the distinction to be made between the two concepts of intelligence and genius, the latter of which has an inherent association to autism. It is commonly said that genius is the product of greater intelligence, but in fact these two concepts are not equivalent at all. From prior discussion, intelligence can be described as the ability to understand and to master the artificial construction contained within the environment, as measured by performance on an IQ exam, the contents of which serve as a proxy for environmental artificial construction. With this in mind, the phrase *greater intelligence* can be taken in two different ways. Within a generational cohort, a person demonstrating more mastery of the existing artificial construction, by scoring better on that cohort's IQ exam, can be described as displaying greater intelligence than his or her peers. And in cohorts separated by time, the later generations, by mastering larger amounts of extant artificial construction—reflected in the additional complexity and variety of later IQ exams—can be described as displaying greater intelligence overall than the earlier generations. But both of these instances of greater intelligence correspond only to greater mastery of the artificial construction *already contained* within the human environment, they do not touch in any way upon the question of how does artificial construction get *inserted* into that environment. For instance, an individual could achieve a better IQ performance than any of his or her peers, and yet contribute nothing further to the environment that would boost later generations. And any generational cohort, while displaying greater overall intelligence than each prior cohort, could then in theory neglect to insert any additional artificial construction into the existing environment, effectively plateauing growth in human intelligence. Therefore, greater intelligence does not account for how new artificial construction gets added into the human environment. For that operation, we must turn to the word *genius*.

Genius does not require greater intelligence. Although an ability to master existing artificial construction certainly can help, the essential requirement for adding new types of artificial construction into the surrounding environment is an ability to discern formations that do not already exist, to perceive structure that no one has perceived before. Over the course of human history, those occasions where humanity's understanding and mastery of its surrounding environment has taken a quantum leap—control of fire, development of agriculture, the Copernican revolution, Newton's laws of motion and gravity, evolutionary theory, the Turing machine, etc.—all these occasions have served to increase the scope and range of humanity's non-biological perception, paving the way to massive advancement in new types of artificial construction. *Genius* is the correct word for describing this process. Genius opens a vista onto a previously unseen world, it breaks the existing mold, it shifts the paradigm. Genius therefore is all about perception, and in particular, all about *atypical* perception. And this is the reason genius has an inherent association to autism.

It is not that biologically typical individuals cannot create products of genius. As stated previously, most human adults today display combined autistic and non-autistic perceptual and behavioral characteristics, and thus a biologically typical individual would have access to the type of perception that can give rise to genius (just as, in the same way, an autistic individual would have access to the type of perception that can give rise to social success). Nonetheless, those individuals who are born autistic have something of a head start and a natural advantage when it comes to producing genius. From their very first days, autistic individuals are continuously perceiving their surroundings in a way that differs from that of most other individuals—that differs, sometimes greatly, from the existing norm—and autistic individuals must often organize their sensory world in a way that can only be described as novel. Thus, atypical perception is the essence of the autistic way of being, and defying the norm is the cornerstone of autistic habit. So when a new vista is to be opened onto the surrounding environment, when the existing mold needs to be broken, when the paradigm has to shift, it can be expected that this process will occur more frequently under an autistically minded influence.

History would appear to provide evidence that this is in fact the case. Those individuals responsible for many of the more famous instances of human genius constitute what can only be described as a rather curious list: Socrates, Archimedes, Newton, Kant, Beethoven, Darwin, Dostoyevsky, Einstein, Turing, and many others. Autism of course was not yet even a concept when most of these individuals lived, and so it would be with some peril and difficulty that we might attempt to apply the term *autism* retroactively to any of these historical figures, an attempt made even more perilous by how poorly we still understand autism today. Nonetheless, the biographies of these individuals have a surprisingly similar character, they are often filled with behavioral terms and descriptions that suggest a degree of separation from the human behavioral norm—eccentric, iconoclastic, awkward, misanthropic, single-minded, odd, isolated—terms and descriptions that in the twenty-first century are frequently associated with autism. This does not constitute definitive proof that autism has been at the heart of these prior instances of human genius, but it does appear to be more than mere coincidence that so many of these influential and genius-producing individuals have also possessed an assortment of autistic-like traits. And at any rate, the hypothesis can still be put to a present and future test. Over the course of the twenty-first century there will be new instances of innovation, new vistas to be opened onto the non-biological structural world, new paradigm shifts. And it will be worth some observation to see how many of these new occasions of genius come also with autism lingering somewhere nearby.

Whether it is looking for evidence of autism's connection to genius, or whether it is attempting to assess autism's impact on the other aspects of human endeavor, an honest and dispassionate observation of autistic individuals and their influence upon the human species would be certainly worth some merit. And yet the greatest current obstacle to actually making these observations is the autism research community itself, which in fact has made very few attempts at such observations over the many years. The autism research community has been too busy, too busy to take time to understand autistic individuals for who they actually are, too busy treating autism as a medical condition, even to the point of cure and eradication. This is the ultimate irony in my opinion, since in my way of perceiving the situation, the entire notion of research itself would be utterly inconceivable without the presence of autistic individuals and the legacy of autistic influence.

The one remaining question is, why humans? Why has the species *Homo sapiens* gained a significant presence of autistic individuals within its population, thereby realizing the impact of that presence, when it would appear no other species has ever experienced a similar circumstance? For that matter, how did humans first gain their own autistic presence, given that such presence seemed to be lacking for quite some time? This is not an easy question to answer, in part because we still do not understand exactly what it is that produces autism. The little that we do know suggests there is a hereditary component to the condition, but whatever the genetic underpinning is, it appears to be general and not at all specific—there is no such thing as an autism gene. So trying to figure out why autism has taken hold in *Homo sapiens*, but in no other species, feels somewhat akin to stumbling about in the dark.

Here would be my suggestion, although I freely admit it to be speculative. It begins with the notion of conspecific distance, a theoretical measure of the amount of separation between two organisms with respect to their ability to achieve conspecific perception for the other. That is, two organisms that have a large conspecific distance between them would also likely have no mutual conspecific perception, whereas two organisms who have a short conspecific distance between them would probably experience a strong degree of conspecific perception. Although there are perhaps many different traits that could contribute to increasing conspecific distance in either or both directions—blindness or deafness in one of the organisms, for instance—I suspect the predominant influence on conspecific distance is the amount of similarity or dissimilarity in each organism's respective genetic makeup. A lion and a leopard, for example, because of their genetic dissimilarity, would have a large amount of conspecific distance between them and therefore no mutual conspecific perception, whereas a lion and a lion would have a small amount of conspecific distance, because the two lions are nearly genetically alike.

But note that even within the same species, there is still going to be a certain amount of conspecific distance between all the members of the population—it is almost never the case that two organisms are genetically the same. So when it comes to achieving a strong degree of conspecific perception, such as that commonly experienced within a given species, a certain amount of conspecific distance can apparently be tolerated. But if conspecific perception remains strong when the conspecific distance is small and yet becomes nonexistent when the conspecific distance is large, this implies that somewhere in between can be found a threshold, an amount of conspecific distance that goes just beyond the toleration limit and begins to produce significant impact upon the ability to achieve conspecific perception. And if we consider the circumstance of an organism being genetically different enough from the other members of its own species to find itself somewhere near or on the other side of that distance threshold, then the consequences are going to be predictable. Such an organism would almost certainly have a weakened sense of conspecific perception relative to the other members of its own species, and this is precisely the circumstance we identified as the primary characteristic of autism.

Assuming that the above description is accurate, it also strongly implies that autism is not unique to humans. It can be expected that any species would at times, due to genetic churn, have members within its population that are conspecifically distant from the others, even to the point of inducing autistic characteristics. Thus, the question becomes not how does autism get introduced into a population—this would appear to be possible for almost any species—but instead, how is it that autism can *take hold* within a population, how does it remain persistent, so that a significant autistic presence can be maintained over time. Autism presents an assortment of survival-and-procreative challenges. Having a weakened sense of conspecific perception means that an organism would have diminished ability to participate successfully in many crucial population activities, activities such as group defense and group hunting. Furthermore, assuming that survival still remains possible despite these many handicaps, an organism with a weakened sense of conspecific perception would then face increased challenges in making a successful sexual connection, decreasing the odds for procreation. Therefore, whatever genetic makeup is responsible for an organism's increased conspecific distance from the other members of its species, the resulting weakening of conspecific perception makes it extremely difficult, if not downright impossible, to propagate those traits. This would explain why autism, although individually possible within almost any species population, nonetheless has almost no chance of obtaining significant and persistent presence within that population.

And this brings us back to the original question—why humans? Why has it been that only in humans, and only quite recently, that autism has managed to gain for itself a significant and persistent presence?

Most animal species produce a large number of offspring. It is a common evolutionary mechanism that each generation will produce a large brood, of which only a small fraction will survive and go on to propagate the next generation. Thus, biologically speaking, for most species, offspring are cheap—their generational value is not with any one individual but is instead with the collective potential of the cohort as a whole. If any one organism finds itself facing an increased survival-and-procreative challenge, there is no population incentive to provide extra care and attention to help that organism along. If it fails to survive and procreate, then so be it, this is nothing more than the expected evolutionary outcome, as it is for so many others.

Also, most types of offspring are born or hatched near the end of their gestational or incubational needs, and come into this world fully ready, or nearly so, to begin fending for themselves. Thus, for most species, relatively little investment is made in the early rearing of helpless young, dampening the loss to be experienced when any one of these offspring turns out to be less viable. So here too, there exists no population incentive to come to the extra aid of any biologically atypical member.

But for hominins the situation is quite different. For hominins, biologically speaking, offspring are expensive, and they have become more expensive over time. Humans generally give birth to only one child at a time, and the total number is limited to only about a dozen over the course of a female's lifespan. So there is already additional incentive to provide extra care and attention to each individual—any one loss can be significant. And furthermore, because of the transition to bipedalism and the resulting narrowing of the birth canal, human children are born quite early relative to their gestational needs, and they come into this world quite helpless, showing first indications of being able to fend for themselves only after the first year or two. Thus, humans make considerable investment in the early rearing of their helpless young, an investment not to be let go of lightly. For these reasons, a *Homo sapiens* child is more likely to be provided with extra support and care so that it might survive and become a participating member of the population, and this remains true no matter what that child's particular situation might happen to be, including the possibility of finding itself conspecifically distanced from the others. It may be that it has been this extra support and care that has provided the initial boost to allow autism to gain its human foothold and to begin consistently propagating its traits. That initial foothold is what is crucial. Once the initial foothold has been achieved, continuation of autism becomes easier over time. One of the more obvious effects of increased artificial construction is that survival and procreation increases greatly for the entire population, so much so that it has vaulted the human count from maybe a hundred thousand not that long ago to a whopping eight billion today. Such an increase in overall survival-and-procreative success helps perpetuate nearly every subpopulation to be found within the species, including the autistic subpopulation.

Whether it has happened by the mechanism as outlined above, or whether it has occurred by some other process, the one thing that is not in doubt is that autistic individuals now constitute a significant and ongoing presence within the human population—at least two percent according to the most recent autism prevalence studies. And there is no reason to think that autistic presence has not been near or at that level for quite some time, meaning there has been ample opportunity over the years for autistic individuals to convey their atypical influence to the remainder of the population.

To summarize the journey we have made:

It began with the observation that the human species is extraordinary. Using Big History for context and perspective, we explored just how unprecedented and large scale the human transformation has been, leading to the remarkable circumstances humanity finds itself in today. But we also noted that much about the human transformation has remained insufficiently explained, and we dubbed these unanswered questions the riddle of humanity.

To begin examining these unanswered questions, we investigated first the concept of biological evolution, the process cited most often when attempting to explain the human transformation. But in fact we found the reality to be just the opposite, that instead of undergoing alteration to fit to a given environment, humanity has reconfigured the evolutionary process, making use of artificial construction to mutate the surroundings to better fit the species' needs—a unique and radical instance of evolution being turned inside out.

Next, we studied artificial construction in greater detail, linking it via the contents of an IQ exam to the topic of human intelligence. A historical investigation further revealed that human intelligence has been consistently increasing as a consequence of the growth in environmental artificial construction, meaning that the Flynn effect has been with humanity for a very long time and is not the result of any neurological alteration, but is instead due entirely to the accumulative environmental construction of intelligence.

We then returned to the question of what has sparked the events of the human transformation—what is it that has catalyzed artificial construction, freedom from evolutionary constraint, and the growth in human intelligence. It was proposed that the answer to this question is the condition known as autism. Because autism is a new concept for humanity and not yet well understood, we took time to explore the condition more deeply. Characterizing autistic individuals as possessing a weakened sense of conspecific perception, weak enough to compel such individuals to adopt a non-biological form of perception to organize their otherwise chaotic sensory world, we settled on this description as being the true nature of autism.

Finally, it was proposed that the significant presence of autistic individuals within the human population has had the impact of bringing non-biological perception to the species as a whole, thereby unleashing all the unprecedented consequences of the human transformation. It was further suggested that the validity of this proposal could be assessed by making careful observation of the impact autistic individuals have upon human perception and human behavior today. These proposals have been offered in the hope of shedding light on the riddle of humanity.

6. Consequences

Humanity finds itself standing between two extremes. On the one hand, there has been no other time in history when humans have experienced so much benefit from the fruits of their transformation. For the vast majority of us, we lack essentially nothing in the way of physical and biological needs and comforts. We have an abundance of food and drink to sustain and to nourish us, so much so that we usually can luxuriate in the broad range of tastes and smells available to our plate and cup. We enjoy nearly complete safety from predators and from the elements, living in dwellings that not only provide us with adequate protection but also give us pleasure and a fulfilling sense of family and community. We engage in sex usually at our leisure and mostly for the sheer delight of it, able to plan procreation for when it is the most convenient. And nearly one hundred percent of our children survive into adulthood, experiencing upbringings full of education and enrichment, eyeing a future that foreseeably will be even better than the one we experience now. We travel with ease, even to the far reaches of the planet. We experience health and lifespans previously unheard of. Compared to the lives of the earliest of *Homo sapiens*, and compared even to the lives of our ancestors from just a few hundred years ago, we live in a near paradise. It washes over us so thoroughly we can easily take it for granted.

In addition, we live in an age where the knowledge and understanding regarding the surrounding environment has reached a nearly unimaginable depth and scope. Quantum mechanics, genetics, artificial intelligence— we seem to be on the verge of obtaining the keys to the entire kingdom, and it is entirely appropriate to think that the universe is somehow coming into consciousness entirely through human means. It is an amazing time to be part of human existence.

But on the other hand, the accelerating pace of change brought forth by the human transformation, along with the immense and growing power of that change—a power that now overwhelms any form of biological defense—this has put humanity into the most precarious of situations. We stand on the precipice of irreversibly ruining the climate for ourselves and for all the other life forms on the planet. We have brought to extinction such a large number of species that we threaten to destroy the balance of life itself. And we have developed and deployed so many weapons of mass destruction that we now have little choice but to merely hope that someone does not pull the decisive trigger and blow the whole thing up. I would liken humanity's current circumstance to that of a teenager driving a souped-up car on county roads, thrilled by the speed, thrilled by the rushing wind, thrilled by the music blaring from the stereo, but racing faster and faster around every bend and swerving more and more erratically from lane to lane. How much longer before careening out of control?

I believe humanity has come to this precarious situation in large part because humanity is lacking two useful pieces of information. One, as claimed at the beginning of this essay, humanity does not as yet understand itself, it does not yet have a grasp on what has caused, and continues to cause, the transformation that has brought this species to its current place. And two, humanity cannot as yet envisage where this transformation might be heading, or what could be its purpose. We are moving ever faster but without knowing why and without knowing which direction we might take.

The value of accurate knowledge and understanding is that it untangles difficulties and provides useful signposts, allowing us to proceed forward with greater control and mastery, with a greater likelihood of taking future actions that will be constructive instead of destructive. Humanity has seen the benefits of this kind of knowledge and understanding in so many different areas—physics, mathematics, engineering, medicine—and if we were to gain a similar level of knowledge and understanding regarding humanity's history and humanity's endeavors, we might come to find that we can proceed forward as a species with greater assurance and much less recklessness, maintaining all the benefits of the human transformation while minimizing the risks.

One place to begin is with a greater awareness—a greater degree of collective consciousness—regarding the dual source of influence that underlies modern humanity. As has been described and emphasized previously, modern humans are to be characterized as being double origined, first as pure animals and then more recently as organisms responsive to the impact of artificial construction. But few humans actually sense or are aware of this dual origin. This may be due in part to the fact that the species has been extremely successful in blending its original influences, giving the overall impression that human perception and behavior operates as a cohesive whole. For example, this blending can be observed in almost every government and corporate institution. These institutions are typically formulated around known patterns of structure, rule and design, and there is a certain degree of objective logic often guiding how these institutions are organized and run. But they are not machines. Weaved among this disinterested structure can be found a broad assortment of activities, protocols, and conventions that are clearly derived more directly from humanity's tribal origins. For instance, there is the totemic importance of the org chart, crucial for knowing who controls what piece of turf and who is to be giving deference to whom. There is the steady hum of gossip around every corner and throughout every channel of communication. There are the countless meetings, even when there is nothing of importance to discuss. And then there is the aphorism about how one manages to get ahead, namely that it is not so much *what* you know as it is *who* you know. These institutions, when stripped down to the motivations that undergird them and allow them to function, can be seen as microcosms of the broad human talent for blending both biological and non-biological influences, of displaying what might be described as an effective mixture of autistic and non-autistic traits.

But I believe the biggest reason that humans are not generally aware of the dual origin of their nature is that they have convinced themselves that human intelligence is innate, that is to say, that human intelligence is predominantly neurological and biological. Thus intelligence, the core characteristic underlying the human transformation, is categorized in the minds of almost everyone as being similar to the rest of the human instincts. We think we have *evolved* our intelligence, instead of having *built* it, and thus we regard our modern perceptions and behaviors as simply a natural extension of our biological and animal selves. But this is a fundamental mistake, a deep misapprehension of who we are and how we operate. It is a self-deluding myth.

The danger of this myth is that it obscures the inherent tension that exists between the two different sources of human influence, between on the one hand the animal aspect of humanity, and on the other hand the constructed aspect of humanity. Despite this species' effectiveness at blending these two aspects when necessary, it still needs to be recognized that in general these two aspects do not always play so well together. They come from entirely different histories and possess entirely different characteristics, and they pull this species in opposite directions. This in turn creates conflict, confusion, turmoil and obstacles to human progress, problems that will not get resolved by misunderstanding what has given rise to them.

The animal aspect of humanity is of course deeply ingrained, and also ever present, because even in the modern era humans must respond to their biological needs and demands. The key word to this aspect is *immediacy*, everything operates in the here and now, and the morality of this aspect is the morality of survival and procreation. But if this seems a bit too brutish and selfish, note also that the animal aspect of humanity has provided much of the vitality spurring this species into productive action. How much artificial construction has been instigated by a personal desire for immediate or near-term gain?

The constructed aspect of humanity, more recent and also constantly shifting, faces the daunting challenge of having to overcome entropy, of having to marshal and to infuse additional amounts of energy and complexity into the existing environment. The key word here is *expansiveness*, an ever-enlarging engagement with time and space. And the morality of this aspect centers around the need to contain the natural urge towards immediacy, a corralling of the beast within. But if this seems a bit too onerous, take another look at the cornucopia of benefit that has been thereby gained, including the most fundamental benefit, that of human freedom. Ask yourself, would we really want to return to the circumstances of being pure animal?

This ongoing tension between these two different aspects of humanity might seem at first to be equally and well met, but this is not entirely accurate. Over the course of human history, one of these aspects has been gaining steadily in ascendency, while the other aspect has been scrambling to retain its relevance. Before the out-of-Africa migration, and even for some time thereafter, the animal aspect of humanity continued to reign supreme. Human life then was still mostly a battle for survival and procreation, even when increasingly aided by the growing influence of artificial construction. But eventually, the constructed aspect of humanity began to take greater and greater control, and today most humans live lives dominated by the artificial construction existing all around them, with their animal selves being little more than appeased. This is a result that seems to be acceptable to many, but it is also a result that seems to be disturbing to some, and I believe a good deal of the pushback against human progress is motivated by a genuine and felt reluctance to let go of our animal selves.

And at any rate, are we even aware of these aspects that are driving our preferences and desires, are we individually and collectively conscious of the history that has forged us into the modern humans we are today? Do we as yet understand ourselves?

As challenging as it can be to understand ourselves today, it is even more difficult to foresee where it is that we might be heading. We could ask, does the human transformation have a purpose or an ultimate goal? Using the context and perspective of Big History, we might ask the same question about all the previous thresholds. The Big Bang, the formation of the chemical elements, the coming together of galactic systems, the origination of life—did these moments have a purpose or an ultimate goal, or were they instead merely a sequence of events connected benignly from one to another? The thing is, these previous events from Big History seem to us to have been predetermined, whereas we feel that humans today have the freedom to make choices. And indeed, from the modern perspective, there are many different directions this species might take:

- We could mindlessly slide into eventual destruction. Much like the teenager driving the souped-up car on county roads, we could just simply enjoy the ride until it finally comes to an end.

- Noting the harm we are doing to the planet and to the other forms of life on Earth, we could magnanimously declare ourselves to be a cancer upon this planet and voluntarily extinct ourselves. This would give Earth the opportunity to heal and to return to its previous evolutionary state.

- Noting the fragility of biology against the power of artificial construction, we could pursue the possibility of non-biological life, employing gained knowledge in physics, robotics, artificial intelligence and the like to create sentient entities more hardy than ourselves. These entities could then continue the process of accruing artificial construction, safe from the risks that come with biological entanglement.

- We could continue in much the same way as we are doing right now, but with greater awareness and a deeper understanding of what has brought us to this place. This would include an appreciation and respect for the needs of our fellow species and for the contributions of autistic individuals.

I admit to being biased, but my personal preference is for the latter choice. I cannot see the advantage of either an eventual destruction or of a voluntary return to an evolutionary past. These paths go backwards in time, to circumstances this universe has already known; I would much rather take the opportunity to experience something new. Plus I am struck by how the depth and breadth of recent understanding—the expansion of knowledge that ranges all the way back to the beginning of time itself, and all the way across the far reaches of space, and all the way down to the most minute of subatomic particles—I am struck by how this deep and growing awareness has the character of the universe coming to consciousness about itself, an occurrence I believe needs to be respected. And finally, I cannot accept the placing of this responsibility into the care of a non-biological entity—I worry there would not be enough vitality to keep the pursuit going and not be enough awe in the presence of its more sublime results.

The human transformation has put our fate into our own hands. This was not always the case. We were once entirely determined and constrained by evolution's rules and bounds, we were not the master of our own destiny. But humans today enjoy freedom from evolutionary constraint, and they have gained the power of artificial construction, and they have the ability to increase their own intelligence. Thus, we humans, whether we like it or not, we are now responsible for ourselves and for our decisions, from which we will reap the inevitable consequences. I believe there is good reason to maintain hope and cheer. By coming to a greater understanding of ourselves and by taking responsibility for our future, we can continue to experience the splendor of that sentence with which this essay began:

The human species, our species, is extraordinary.

Printed in the United States
by Baker & Taylor Publisher Services